LANYA LYNN ELSA, PhD
WITH ALEE ANDERSON

SILENCE

and

Light

A Mother's Journey of
Self-Discovery Through Advocacy

Revised Edition

Published by As You Wish Publishing
Medford, Oregon
www.asyouwishpublishing.com

ISBN: 979-8-9910499-3-1

This revised edition includes updated content, a newly added chapter, and reflects the author's name change from Lanya McKittrick, PhD. to Lanya Lynn Elsa, PhD.

First edition published in 2024. Revised edition published in 2025.
Printed in the United States of America

Praise for Silence and Light

A powerful story of motherly love and the resilience of families.

A mother's life turns upside down following her child's diagnosis with a rare genetic disorder in McKittrick's debut memoir.

The book opens with the author reflecting on her career ambitions and early marital bliss with her husband Todd as they relished the upcoming birth of their first child. ("I loved every second of being pregnant," she recalls.) After she gave birth, it became clear early on that something was amiss with their newborn son, Conner, who was no longer attracted to the bright colors and sounds he had initially been drawn to. The instant their pediatrician told the McKittricks, "Your son is profoundly deaf," the author writes, "my life changed." The career and personal ambitions that were such a driving force in the book's opening chapter "weren't important anymore"—McKittrick would devote the next 25 years of her life to taking care of her son.

Conner was diagnosed with a rare genetic disorder called Usher syndrome, a disease that left him both deaf and blind. Despite undergoing genetic embryo screening for their fourth child, Dalton, he too would be diagnosed with Usher syndrome in his early childhood. Much of the narrative centers on the McKittricks' journey through the medical system (Conner's first doctor downplayed early warning signs) and the ways in which the disease impacts the lives of children.

The strength of the book lies in the author's openness about her own "trauma," a word she never associated with herself until going to therapy years later. While privately enduring internalized grief, she "felt substantial societal pressure to put on a 'brave face,'" McKittrick notes.

The author's story is also one of proactively taking on life's challenges, as McKittrick would eventually receive a doctorate from the University of North Colorado—her award-winning dissertation focused on the education of deafblind children. She also cofounded the Hear See Hope Foundation, which funds research, advocacy, and awareness campaigns for Usher syndrome. The book's honest, intimate narrative concludes with advice for mothers navigating rare genetic diagnoses, encouraging them to "Use self-care in the face of trauma."

A powerful story of motherly love and the resilience of families.

Kirkus Review

This book is honest, inspirational, and encouraging!

Thank you for writing this book! It is an honest and inspirational account of the struggles of motherhood and the strong motivation to offer our children the best opportunities available. I appreciate the relatable and often humorous accounts of pregnancy and motherhood. We all face struggles as parents, and this book encouraged me to set priorities to care for my children and myself in the best way possible. I highly recommend this book to all parents, especially those dealing with medical and mental health challenges.

Carrie

Captivating and Moving!

Lane's story is a testament to the boundless love and unwavering advocacy of a mother determined to give her family the best life with love and through unwavering advocacy. Removing barriers, challenging the norms, educating some folks while holding others accountable, and creating community for those families who need support and resources - these are just a few of Lane's powerful actions you'll read about. Raw honesty and emotional depth will captivate the reader, and the undeniable thread of hope and resilience will keep them turning pages. Anyone seeking a deeper understanding of the human spirit and the capacity to endure and overcome will love this memoir. Even in uncertain, difficult, frustrating, and sometimes dark times, light can be found. Thank you for sharing your story of the trials and triumphs of raising children with rare genetic conditions - you are truly empowering, Lane.

Heather

Inspiring and Heartfelt

I couldn't put it down! Silence and Light is a beautiful story that demonstrates a mother's love for her family. Your boys are blessed to have you, just like you are blessed to have them!!

Juli

Written from the Heart

As a fellow Special Ed Mama, I was waiting for Lanya's book. It was refreshing to read about a fellow Mom struggle and overcome obstacles. It can be lonely being a Mom with a child finding their way and after reading the book, I realized I am not alone. Bravo and I hope

Lane continues to write and share her story. This was an easy read and I could not put it down!

T.S.

Very Interesting and Important

I couldn't put it down!! As a special ed. Teacher, I appreciated her perspective and concerns from a parents point of view. I didn't understand fully how tough and lonely the journey could have been. But your boys are lucky to have you.

Joyce

A Powerful Memoir that's Hard to Put Down!

Silence and Light by Lanya McKittrick is a powerful memoir that delves into the author's journey as a mother of two children diagnosed with a rare genetic condition, Usher syndrome. Through this deeply personal narrative, Dr. McKittrick explores the emotional complexities of parenting a child with disabilities, including grief, advocacy, and ultimately self-discovery.Dr. McKittrick recounts her experiences navigating the medical system, searching for resources, and building a supportive community. Her story is both heartbreaking and inspiring, as it highlights the challenges and triumphs of advocating for a child with special needs while finding strength within herself. The book also offers valuable lessons on resilience, hope, and the importance of community, especially for families facing similar struggles.I was moved by Lane's honesty about the emotional toll of parenting a child with disabilities, while also finding hope in her message of perseverance and advocacy. It's an uplifting read for anyone interested in themes of disability, special education, and the human capacity for growth in the face of adversity. She continues to be an inspiration to me.

Kristen

Intelligent, Heartfelt, Important

Lanya's story is not just inspiration but important: it's a transparent look into what it means to be a parent of children with disabilities. Her words are beautiful, heart wrenching, and all together moving.

Rebecca

Dedication

I dedicate this book to my kids, Conner, Cole, Hunter, and Dalton, who have each played a unique role in shaping my perspective on disability and family, and to Todd: thank you for your steadfast support and for traveling this journey with me. We've raised some amazing kids.

This journey wouldn't have been possible without all of you by my side.

Silence and Light

By Lanya Lynn Elsa, PhD

A Note to the Reader: Your Companion on This Journey

When I first wrote Silence and Light, I had no idea how deeply it would resonate—not just with parents of children with disabilities, but with anyone who has ever had to navigate the unexpected. Over time, I heard from readers who said, "I wish I had space to process everything I felt while reading," or "I want to read this with others, but I'm not sure where to start."

So in this updated edition, I've included something special—a Companion Guide. It's filled with questions and prompts to help you reflect, journal, or discuss as you move through the book.

Some questions are universal—about loss, identity, resilience, and finding your voice. Others are specific to parents navigating systems and raising children with unique needs. You can use this guide on your own, in a group, or even in a therapeutic setting.

An abbreviated version of the guide is included in the back of the book for quick reference. If you'd like the full printable version—with journaling space, group discussion suggestions, and chapter-by-chapter prompts—you can download it for free at:

www.lanyaelsa.com/silenceandlightcompanionguide Or scan the QR code at the end of this book.

You don't have to answer every question. You don't have to go in order.

Just let it meet you where you are. Use what serves you, and skip what doesn't.

More than anything, I hope this guide reminds you that you are not alone. You are not "too much" for needing space to feel. You are not "behind" for still figuring things out. You are human. And your story—just like mine—is worthy of reflection, healing, and light.

With love and solidarity,

Lanya Lynn Elsa

Contents

Introduction

There are moments in life that split you open. Moments that shake the foundation you thought you were standing on and ask you to rebuild—brick by careful brick—with more honesty than before. This book was born from one of those moments.

When I first began writing Silence and Light, I was a mother who had been navigating the complex and often isolating world of parenting children with disabilities for twenty-five years. Two of my sons had been diagnosed with Usher syndrome, a rare condition that causes deafblindness. Writing was a way for me to make sense of the overwhelming grief, the nonstop medical appointments, and the pressure to always be "on"—to always know what to do.

What started as a way to process the grief and fear became something bigger. It became a reflection of motherhood in all its rawness. Of the invisible labor of caregiving. Of the quiet strength it takes to advocate when your voice is shaking. And also of the moments of light—small, tender, sacred moments that reminded me I wasn't alone.

This new edition holds all of that and more. Over time, I've come to understand that while the external circumstances of our lives matter, it's the internal transformation that truly shapes us. What you'll find in these pages is a story of both—a mother navigating systems and diagnoses and a woman slowly remembering who she is beyond the roles she's been asked to carry.

I've learned that we're allowed to evolve. That grief and joy can live side by side. That even in the messiest moments, we can choose to listen to the quiet voice inside—the one that says there's more for you, too.

This book is for the parents who wake up exhausted and still keep going. It's for the caregivers who wonder if anyone really sees how hard they're trying. It's for the professionals who care deeply, who are still learning, and who want to show up with more heart. And it's for anyone who has ever asked themselves, "Am I allowed to want more?"

You are. You always have been.

This story is about silence. About the kind that follows a diagnosis. The kind that settles in after everyone else goes home. But it's also about light—the kind that breaks through when you least expect it. The kind that reminds you: even here, especially here, you are becoming.

Welcome.

One

I STOOD IN THE nursery in a golden ray of sunlight that streamed in through a crack in the gauzy, blue curtains. Butterflies came to life in my belly as my eyes wandered around the room. It filled my heart to see the wide array of things we'd been gifted for sweet baby Conner now placed meticulously along the walls. There was a shelf packed with books, a changing table positioned in the corner, a beautiful light wood crib with crisp-fitted sheets, a red, black, and white-colored mobile above his bed, a dozen special toys from friends and family arranged just so, and a rocking chair, the one I had carefully picked out, facing the window. This room—my happy place—was filled to the brim with love.

I leaned forward and placed a CD in the blue clock radio that sat on the bookshelf. I closed it and rested my hands on my swollen belly as it started to whir. Classical music swelled, draping itself around my body as I began to sway.

The music rose.
Kick, kick.
The music fell.
Kick, kick.

Kick.

Kick, kick.

I giggled.

Listening to music with Conner was one of my favorite things to do—it made me feel so connected to him, like he was already there in my arms. Each day, I'd play our favorite songs and move my body to the beat. Sometimes he'd sleep through it; other times, he'd wiggle, and today he was all big kicks and punches. I reveled in this feeling of pure joy. It was as though I'd entered motherhood already and was parenting like a pro. I laughed as he kicked again, adjusting my hands and rubbing circles on my belly.

"You're so silly, Conner! Great dancing!"

I turned the music down as I kept rubbing in circles. I gazed past the curtains and out over our lush lawn, toward the mature trees that bordered the property. We'd recently moved from a condominium in downtown Seattle, and I was soaking in every facet of suburban life in our first house. I drew a deep breath as I tuned into the sound of waxy leaves billowing in the breeze, rubbing together with soft *tap, tap, taps.* I listened to the quiet chirping of birds and thought for a moment about how lucky I was. At thirty-seven weeks pregnant, most women find themselves ready for their pregnancy to be over. They roll their eyes and groan things like "I'm just so over this!" and "I can't wait to get this baby out!"

Not me. I loved every second of being pregnant—so much so that it felt bittersweet to see it come to an end.

I was lucky in that way; my body handled pregnancy well. I was fortunate to never have dealt with any of the awful symptoms so many women experience. My back never hurt. I never felt nauseous. I never got angry stretch marks or big, swollen feet. Instead, I felt strong. I felt happy. I felt excited. I felt *good*.

I felt so good in fact that I still insisted on mowing the lawn, my favorite chore. Todd worried that the neighbors would think he was forcing his pregnant wife to do manual labor; I sometimes chuckled as I made my way around the grass, thinking about curtains twitching, as our neighbors looked on, wide-eyed as I pushed the cumbersome mower around the yard.

I watched as a sparrow swooped onto the grass, grabbed a worm, and flitted away. I thought about him heading back to his nest and feeding it to his brood of baby birds, peeping and squawking for more. My mind drifted to Todd and all the reasons I knew he'd be an amazing dad. He already was—he loved Conner and me so well.

It's funny how life works. When I met Todd, barely two years earlier, I certainly didn't think he was *the one*. There were no lightning bolts, no immediate signs, no instant, zingy feeling of love. In fact, if I'm completely honest, I didn't like him much at all.

It was Valentine's Day when Todd visited my office with a friend to learn about our company and the real estate construction projects we had in the works. My boss called me over the intercom and asked me to bring in a set of blueprints for a project I had been working on. I'll never forget how Todd was sitting in the small conference room in a dress shirt and pleated khakis the day we first met.

I came into the conference room and sat down at the table across from him and we shared about the project. I entered the room annoyed. I'd been in the middle of a big financial analysis, and this meeting had interrupted my progress, a meeting I wasn't even sure why I'd been asked to be part of. When it drew to a close, Todd gave me a strange look, and it was then that I realized what he thought.

I stared back at him, my brow wrinkled.

I had a notebook with me, but was jotting notes for myself—they were chicken scratch.

I looked around the room at the other staff members—all men.

I stared back at Todd and cocked my head.

I realized at that moment that he thought I was the admin.

I was actually the president of the company.

What a jerk.

After a few weeks, my boss told me that he had hired Todd as a project manager for the sister company that would be doing the construction on the residential home building projects we were developing. We'd be forced to work together.

Shocker: it didn't go well.

No matter what we did, we couldn't seem to get on the same page. He was a construction guy, and I was a finance person, and we never saw eye-to-eye. Our conversations were short and clipped, our interactions peppered with sighs and eye rolls. We just... didn't click.

Then, one Saturday, I was out doing errands when I drove past his office on the way to pick something up from mine. The parking lot was empty except for his SUV, which was parked in his usual spot by the door. I had to admit: he was dedicated to the project. I appreciated seeing him there alone on a weekend, his nose to the grindstone.

I navigated my car into the parking lot and slid into the spot next to his. I made my way inside the dim office and found him at his desk, working in the warm glow of lamplight.

"Funny seeing you here," I called out.

"Yeah," he chuckled. "My boss is a real hard-ass."

I rolled my eyes and shook my head.

We talked about the project, how things were going, and what our completion date looked like. Soon, we had moved on to talking about nothing, really—maybe the weather, maybe something else—but, before I knew it, we were laughing, both of us finally dropping our guards. It struck me how incredibly down-to-earth he seemed. When we finished chatting, I said my goodbyes and left for my office. As I entered, the phone was ringing. It was Todd on the other end: "Are you free for dinner tonight?" That night, we sat across the table from one another at Il Bistro, an Italian restaurant under Pike Place Market, learning about each other's lives, hopes, and dreams. After that fateful dinner, things moved quickly.

We spent a lot of time together. I thought we were dating, but he insists to this day that we were not; he struggled with mixing business with pleasure. Long story short, after a confusing few months of non-dating dating, we officially became a couple. Once we cleared up that he really did think I was the admin when we first met and agreed to disagree on our approach to business, we became inseparable.

We moved in together the very next month, were engaged the month after that, and were married less than a year after. I especially loved how he could make me laugh. We wanted a big family and decided we didn't want to wait, so we started to try for a baby. It was barely two months before I came out of the bathroom holding a pregnancy test, my lips pressed together, tears welling in the corners of my eyes. He wrapped me in a tight hug and whispered in my ear, "I can't wait."

Todd and I tackled pregnancy together, our hands interlocked every step of the way. Todd joyfully read *What to Expect When You're Expecting for Dads* and devoured every other pregnancy and parenting book I brought home. He even endured a session of classes I asked him to take—Dad Baby Camp—hosted by the hospital for expecting dads. He came to every doctor's appointment and spent evenings in bed next to me, sweetly talking to Conner through my growing belly. He'd kiss my cheek as Conner kicked, and he kicked a lot—especially after I'd downed one of my favorite treats, a blue Slurpee from 7-11. I always joked that Todd spent so much time there for me that he should've been paying rent—all I had to do was give him *the look*, wide-eyed with a small smirk, and he'd be on his way. As soon as the straw was in my mouth, Conner and I were happy, and Todd was grinning ear-to-ear. We were already a family, the three of us. We were the Three Musketeers.

I smiled to myself in the nursery, letting the memories fade into the ether and refocusing on Conner's sweet wiggles. As the music faded, I eased myself onto the rocker and grabbed a book from the shelf. I pulled the handle on the side of the chair and let the leg rest come up from beneath my tired legs. I cracked the spine on the brand-new book, and began to read, softly.

"Your Mommy loves you; my bunny, I do."

I rubbed my belly.

"Millions of kisses I have just for you."

I rubbed my belly.

"My heart's full of love that blossoms and grows."

I rubbed my belly.

"From your little nose to those teensy toes."

I rubbed my belly.

"*I love you, sweet Conner,*" I whispered. "*I can't wait to meet you.*"

Two days later, Todd and I lay on the couch together in the pulsing glow of the TV. I was startled the second I felt a warm gush of fluid between my legs; at thirty-seven weeks, we thought we had a little more time.

Panic set in as I felt my belly tighten. It released, then tightened again. Then again. And again. Soon, there was dull pain along with the tightening sensations, and Todd dialed the doctor's number as I scrambled to my feet. He ran into the kitchen and grabbed the first thing he saw: a roll of paper towels. He ran back out into the living room and thrust them between my legs. Unsure of what to do next, I waddled to the car, straddling a fistful of them.

We raced to the hospital and ran inside. I wasn't having any major contractions yet, but my water had broken, so I knew it was time.

Conner was on his way, but I wasn't quite ready—*we* weren't ready. The hospital staff got me into a bed and administered medicine to slow my labor, with a plan to induce me the next morning. I somehow managed to get some sleep that night with Todd on a stiff, faux leather chair next to me. His hand never left mine.

The next morning, my doctor came into the room flanked by two nurses.

"Are you ready to have a baby?" she asked.

Having settled into the idea of it being time to meet my son, I nodded excitedly. I'd spent months preparing for a natural childbirth, and I was ready to endure the miracle of labor and delivery. As they administered Pitocin, I laughed to myself and thought of my Slurpees—the date happened to be July 11th (7/11).

With the Pitocin dripping, I lay back, clutching Todd's hand. The contractions came on fast and furious, and before I knew it, the pain was so excruciating that I felt like I was being ripped in two. It was the kind of pain that makes you bite your cheeks until you taste copper—the kind that threatens to bring you to your knees and make you howl at the moon. Soon, I was begging for medicine.

"Please, give it to me now!" I cried. But things were moving too fast.

It was almost too late, but they made it—just barely. Soon, my contractions were bleeding together, the pressure rising and falling like roiling ocean waves. I braced myself.

"I have to push!" I yelled.

"Push now!" The doctor called out in response.

I pushed once.

I pushed again.

I cried out.

I pushed once more.

And Baby Conner slid into the world.

There was a flurry of activity in the room as the doctor lifted him, his pink body wrinkled and wriggling. He was perfect and round with a full head of brown hair. He immediately let out a piercing wail—the most beautiful sound in the world. I laughed as tears slid down my face, my body heaving between sobs. Todd leaned over me and wrapped me in a hug.

"You did it, babe," he said. "He's here."

I let out a wail as I reached my arms out. The nurse handed Conner over to me, wiping off the vernix and traces of blood and fluid. Tears rolled down my cheeks as I looked down into his wide eyes.

"Hi, buddy," I whispered. "I'm your mom." Todd leaned in.

"Hey, buddy, it's me—Daddy. We've spent a long nine months waiting for you."

I kissed the top of Conner's head, my lips grazing his still-wet mop of hair. The nurse leaned forward and placed a hat on him. I lifted him higher and kissed his forehead before resting his soft cheek on my shoulder.

Now, this—this was *love*.

Our time in the hospital sped by, as it tends to do when you bring a healthy baby into the world. Todd was there every step of the way, his chin covered in stubble and eyes sleepy but filled with a delirious love. There was a constant stream of nurses and doctors in and out of the room, each one there to check on Conner and me for various reasons. I soon got acclimated to breastfeeding, which Conner took to easily. I settled into late night diaper changes and singing sweet lullabies. Before we knew it, we were clumsily strapping Conner into his car seat and packing up the bag of *essentials* I brought and barely touched. Todd clipped Conner's car seat into its base, and I slid next to our baby boy in the backseat. As Todd expertly navigated the twists and turns on our short ride home, I sat with Conner's little fingers tightly wrapped around mine. He blinked up at me with his wide, brown eyes as if to say: "I love you, Mommy. Never let me go."

We settled into a routine fairly quickly, and Todd and I enjoyed every zingy moment of the early days of parenthood. I was up most nights with Conner, breastfeeding and changing diapers by the light of the moon. Then, I'd settle back into bed with Conner on my chest, letting out soft sighs as he slept. Todd would ease himself out of bed in the morning and gently lift Conner from his warm spot on top of me. He'd take him into the living room so I could finally roll over and rest, my body snuggled into a tight ball. When I'd wake, I'd wander sleepy-eyed into the living room to be with my boys. Todd would call out, "Look, it's Mommy!" and I'd take Conner into my arms.

As the weeks turned into months, we excitedly learned every facet of our little baby's developing personality. He especially loved when we'd make big facial expressions and give him warm, sweet kisses. I'd sit in front of him and cover my face with my hands and say,

"Aaaaahhhhhhhhhhhh, PEEK-A-BOO!"

His face would light up and he'd squeal, his tiny lips curling into one of those gummy, new baby smiles. He was moved by anything big and bright with music in the background—he especially loved Baby Mozart videos, which were packed with vibrant colors, moving shapes, and songs that filled the room. When those videos were on, he'd become quiet and still, staring into the screen like nothing else existed in the world. As the images shifted, he'd kick, punch, and coo. Those moving shapes, they moved *him*.

We soon began to learn that Conner was a particularly attached baby who loved nothing more than the loving touch of his parents, and he loved Mommy's touch most of all. When my hands were on him, he was so calm, nestling into softness and serenity. Anytime I moved my hands, he would wake with a start and cry out as if to say, "Mommy, where are you? Where *are* you?" He'd scream until his little face turned purple, only settling once my hand was back in his palm or resting on his head or chest. He'd shudder before calming himself as I placed my face.

"Shhhhh, buddy," I'd whisper. *"Shhhhhhhhh. Mommy's here."*

Todd and I found ways to adjust, accommodating all of Conner's little baby quirks. We staged the house so he had places to rest, sleep, and play where I could settle comfortably next to him. I moved from station to station all day long, and Todd and I shared a lot of laughs about our parenting skills. It was only a matter of weeks before I dropped the expectation that I could do laundry, dishes, or really anything while I was on Conner duty alone. It just wasn't feasible, and that was okay.

Conner's attachment never waned, so we quickly gathered everything we needed to safely co-sleep, reasoning that it was better for him to sleep with us than to not sleep at all. I'd snuggle up next to him in bed and place my hand on his chest, feeling his tiny heartbeat. He'd sigh and close his eyes, making tiny peeps as he slept. If I had to get up and go to the bathroom, I'd nudge Todd, who would swiftly rest his hand on Conner's chest in place of mine. Our baby was particular, but we made it work.

Things got much easier once we introduced the greatest invention of all time: a Baby Bjorn. I began wearing Conner in the front carrier nearly all the time, his head pressed firmly against my chest and tiny fingers clutching the tangled ends of my brown hair. If we had to go anywhere in the car, I'd place him in his car seat and jog to the driver's seat as he cried. I'd strap myself in and reach behind me with one hand, holding onto his so he knew I was still there. My shoulder ached all the time, but it was worth it. He knew I was there with him—always.

Conner's love of closeness became a hallmark of our parenting journey. The three of us would cuddle in bed with Conner resting on my chest, and he'd go limp in those moments, letting out soft sighs. He'd bob his head, constantly searching for my breast, trying to be as close as he possibly could. Whenever I'd sit up to get comfortable, he'd nuzzle into me and feed until my skin was raw and bleeding. He ate so much that he gained weight at a rapid rate—he was in the 99th percentile at every doctor's visit. He'd grip my chest, tug at my hair, and push himself into me—so snuggly that it was as though he wished he could go back inside. I never stopped to wonder about his attachment because, as challenging as it was, it felt like love.

Of course, it was love.
But it was also something more.

Two

Light poured through the sheer blue curtains in Conner's room as he started to sleep, his little chest rising and falling with each breath. I ran my fingers over his plump cheeks and smiled softly at him. At four months old, he was just as attached as ever, still screaming anytime I wasn't nearby; when I was, he'd clench my fingers in his fist so tightly his tiny dimpled knuckles would turn white. He also continued to feed ravenously around the clock, leaving my brain foggy and my flesh raw and wounded. But this was all par for the course, I reasoned. Todd and I knew early parenthood would be tricky, and it certainly was, but we were making it work like champions.

With Conner asleep, it was time to get the house back in order. It never failed to amaze me how much of a mess we could make in a few short hours. Thanks to my obsessive neatening before bedtime, we'd always wake to a neat and orderly house. Then, by the time we reached morning naptime, it looked like a tornado had kicked up in the kitchen and eaten its way through our home again. There were used burp cloths, nursing pillows, blankets, pacifiers, pillows, and small squeaky toys everywhere. It was insane. Putting the chaos out of my mind, I took a deep breath and a slug of coffee and got started.

The good thing was, I had gotten my process down to a science. I grabbed a laundry basket and quickly tossed all of the dirty laundry into it, placed it on top of the washing machine, and began throwing toys back into their bins. Once I folded the blankets and put the pillows back into their places, I hurried into the kitchen, placed the dishes in the dishwasher, and wiped the counters down. My hands still wet, I made my way down the hallway to check on Conner. He was still sound asleep, his little hands balled into fists as his tiny lips sucked the air. I had some extra time, so I padded over to the hall closet and tugged the vacuum out of it. I swept strands of hair out of my face as I ran the vacuum over the living room floor and into the entryway before staring down the hallway and pressing my lips into a tight line. The hallway desperately needed to be vacuumed, but I knew if I did it, I'd need to prepare myself for Conner to wake up screaming. Desperate to get my daily chores completed, I took a deep breath and pushed the vacuum down the hallway, sucking up dust as fast as I could. Once I made it to the end of the hallway and turned back, I switched the vacuum off, bracing for Conner's piercing wails.

Silence.

I smiled to myself and switched the vacuum back on. I was going to take this miracle as a win. As I approached Conner's door with the vacuum, I peeked inside through a crack in the door, chewing my bottom lip as I watched him. His little eyes twitched: still asleep. I counted *one, two, three* in my head and pushed the door open wider; I knew I was pushing my luck, but I had to try. I pushed the vacuum around Conner's room—around the glider, up to the bookshelf, and then under his crib. I made it out of his bedroom in two minutes flat, switched the vacuum off, and did a little happy dance. I couldn't believe how lucky I'd gotten. My sweet little buddy had let me get through my chores in time to enjoy a cup of coffee outside with a chilly fall breeze ruffling my hair.

When Todd arrived home that evening, I met him at the door with Conner in my arms. "Hi, Daddy!" I said.

"Hi, you two! How was the day?"

"Todd, it was awesome. You won't believe it—during Conner's morning nap, I was able to get *everything* done that I wanted to do around here, including *vacuuming*. Can you believe it? This amazing baby slept right through it. I even went into his room!"

"Wow! That's great, buddy!" Todd said. He reached for Conner, taking him from my arms and kissing his head as he let out a soft cry.

Over the next few weeks, vacuuming while Conner slept became part of my routine. I'd breeze in and out of his room casually, taking my time as I worked the vacuum into every corner. Conner was such a deep sleeper that he never flinched as I cleaned—it was the most miraculous thing I had ever seen. Then, one evening, Todd and I stood in the kitchen chatting while he prepared dinner. Conner was asleep in a nearby bouncy chair, his tiny feet rubbing together. My breath caught as Todd knocked a pot off the counter with a loud *clunk!* I squished my eyes shut as I waited for Conner's sharp scream... but nothing came. I began to laugh as I opened my eyes and saw Todd standing there frozen with a smirk on his face.

"That was lucky!" he said.

"I know!" I replied. "I just can't believe what a deep sleeper he is."

"I can't believe it. A freight train could roll through here, and he'd sleep through it. I mean, look..."

Todd picked up the pot and banged it on the sink. Conner didn't flinch, and we both folded into laughter. He picked up a pot in each hand and banged them together. Conner still didn't flinch. I clapped and stomped, laughing so hard my stomach ached. But the laughter soon faded, and I scrunched my eyebrows together.

"Todd," I asked hesitantly, "do you think this is normal?" I narrowed my eyes and walked over to the bouncer and snapped my fingers next to Conner's ear—first the left, then the right. Nothing. "I don't know, Todd. He isn't even stirring."

"I'm sure he's all right, he's just—"

Before Todd could finish, Conner let out a soft cry. I leapt forward and scooped him up out of the bouncer and pulled him into me. The tension left my body as relief washed over me. *He's fine.* I thought. *He's just sleeping hard. That's all.* In the coming days, however, I couldn't shake the thought that something wasn't quite right.

I found myself obsessed with trying to wake Conner with loud noises, often walking into his room with a pot and a spoon, banging the pot and waiting for a reaction. No matter what I did, he remained asleep, softly snoring despite the racket I was making. It soon dawned on me that Conner didn't startle to sound when he was awake, either; I could turn on a blender, let out a loud sneeze, or turn the TV up loud without him reacting at all. The only time he seemed to startle was by an unexpected touch, which would make him jump wildly, arms and legs jutting out at all angles, eyes wide as saucers. But that wasn't all.

Todd and I had also begun noticing that Conner's progression wasn't quite lining up with the baby books we'd read. We were hurdling toward his six-month checkup and he still wasn't rolling over, pushing up, or supporting himself with his arms. We'd noticed a bit of a lag over time, but his weight and length were off the charts, so we assumed his slower progress was because he had so much weight to work with. Soon, however, I began to wrestle with a theory.

Conner had frequently suffered with awful ear infections. He'd claw at his ears, his face so red it was nearly purple, screaming so loud his voice would go hoarse. The infections were so frequent that we became regulars at the doctor's office, with a nurse dutifully checking his ears and sighing, "Yep—Mom, we've got another one." I began to wonder if somehow his ear infections were linked to the fact that he wasn't startling to sound—maybe it was somehow impacting his hearing?

The sky was dishwater gray on the day of Conner's six-month checkup. I unclipped his car seat and hoisted it out of the car as Todd jogged ahead and pulled the office door open for us. We followed a nurse back into an exam room where I undressed Conner and placed a dry diaper on him. All done, I carried him out to a smaller room where the nurse smiled and said, "Okay, Mom, if you'll just pop him onto the scale for me here." I had to pry Conner's fingers off of me as he began to scream.

"It's okay, Conner," I said. "I'm not going anywhere. This'll be super quick." The nurse raised her eyebrows and smiled as she stared at the scale.

"Big boy!" she exclaimed.

She led me back to the room where I sat next to Todd, who bounced Conner on my knee. We waited for nearly an hour, flinching at the sound of children screaming through blood draws and vaccines being administered in nearby rooms. Finally, we heard footsteps outside and the rustling of paper. Then, a sharp knock on the door as it opened and Dr. Riley stepped inside, walking directly to the sink to wash his hands.

"Mr. and Mrs. McKittrick, it's good to see you."

"It's good to see you too," I said with a half-smile.

Dr. Riley rolled a stool in front of us and sat down with a *rattle*. He gripped Conner's file in his hands and flipped through the pages.

"Looks like length and weight are off the charts—that's excellent," he said, placing his stethoscope in his ears and warming the chest piece between his hands. "How is everything else going?"

"Things are going well, but we have a few concerns," Todd replied.

"Concerns?"

"Yes," I said, stroking Conner's legs as he tried to wiggle away from the stethoscope. "We've noticed that Conner isn't startling—or even really reacting—to loud noises at all. We can vacuum, bang pots and pans, really anything, and he doesn't react. He'll react to a surprising touch, but that's about all."

"Okay," Dr. Riley replied, reaching for his otoscope, which was tethered to the wall by a curly cord.

"We really just want to make sure everything's all right," Todd added. "As you know, he gets these ear infections…"

"Well, nothing looks out of the ordinary," Dr. Riley said, adjusting the otoscope. "Ear infections aren't abnormal." He sat up and looked from me to Todd and back again, his deep wrinkles accentuated as he furrowed his brow.

"What if there's something going on we don't know about?" I asked.

"Exactly," Todd added again. "He's also behind in hitting his milestones. He isn't rolling over or anything like that."

"Milestones aren't an exact science," Dr. Riley replied. "There is a lot of leeway in those estimates. With his hearing, even if there is an issue, there really isn't anything to be done. He could have hearing loss, but it wouldn't do us any good to know that at this stage. Let's just not worry about anything and see how we're doing at our next visit."

I found myself nodding.

"Great," he continued. "The nurse will be in to get those vaccines taken care of. Good to see you." With that, Dr. Riley pushed his stool back and breezed out of the room.

Later that afternoon, weary from the appointment and the aftermath of the vaccines, I sat on the couch with Todd as Conner slept.

"This doesn't feel right," I said, rubbing my eyes.

"It really doesn't," he replied. "I can't imagine going another few months like this. We need to know if something is going on—for Conner's sake and ours."

"I just can't believe the doctor didn't say anything helpful. It was like he didn't care. Did he even listen to what we said?"

"I don't know, but we need to do something."

I jumped from the couch and dialed the doctor's office. I didn't care what Dr. Riley thought. We were going to take Conner to see a specialist as soon as we possibly could.

I drew a breath as I propped Conner on my lap, bouncing my knees to calm him as he squirmed. The soundproof room was silent save the low chatter of two audiology assistants standing in the doorway, prepping for the more formal hearing exam Conner was about to undergo. Soon, the assistants took their seats facing me, one to my left, one to my right. The room was dark and the walls black, with little marionettes hanging in each corner. The audiologist explained that throughout the test period, they'd play a series of noises at varying volume levels. As each one played, they'd observe how Conner reacted. The marionettes in each corner would dance as a reward as he glanced in the direction of each sound, one by one. My mind wandered to the pots and pans, and I chewed the inside of my cheeks. Finally, the assistant with a blond flippy ponytail leaned forward.

"Okay, Mom, can you sit Conner in the high chair?" she asked.

"He can't sit up on his own yet," I said, swallowing hard.

"It's okay," the assistant with curly brown hair piped up. "He's fine in your lap."

"We ready?" the audiologist asked over the speaker from the sound booth.

"We're ready," I said, trying to remain perfectly still as Conner wiggled.

"Let's get started," the other assistant chirped.

The door closed.

The first sound came from the right corner.

Ding!

Conner stared straight ahead. Then, a sound from the left corner.

Pop!

Conner stared at the floor.

Ding!

Beep!

DING, DING!

Conner stared ahead, and the marionettes stayed still.

The audiologist started turning the marionettes on, causing their limbs to wiggle clumsily, trying to see if Conner just wasn't understanding the task at hand—yet nothing anyone did made any difference at all. Conner remained relaxed on my lap, not paying any attention to the sounds or reacting to the activity.

Fifteen minutes later, the lights came up. Conner kicked and wiggled, staring at the bulbs as they brightened. The blond assistant led me out into the hallway where I met Todd, and we walked together to the audiologist's office. My palms were sweaty, my throat dry as we each took a seat on one of the hard chairs in front of her desk. I quickly positioned Conner and let him latch onto my breast beneath my oversized shirt.

"Did he do okay?" Todd asked.

"I'm not sure, I—"

The door opened and the audiologist walked in. Her curly brown hair hung to her shoulders and a pair of gold-rimmed glasses were propped on her nose.

"Hi there, I'm Dr. Blackwood," she said, shaking Todd's hand and nodding at me as I continued to nurse. "Thank you so much for coming in today."

"Thank you for seeing us so soon," I said. "We've been really nervous about all this."

"Absolutely. I know how stressful it can be when concerns like this arise. Having looked at Conner's results, I can say that it does appear that he has some hearing loss—but to what extent, we can't really say." Todd squeezed my knee. "As you may have guessed, it's not easy with a six-month-old to know exactly what we're seeing in the sound booth. Sometimes their responses, or lack thereof, just don't give us a good indication. We saw some cause for concern in Conner's test, but I can't say with certainty what exactly is going on. I'm therefore going to suggest that you take some additional steps."

"We'll do anything. We just want answers," I said, my face hot.

"Yes, just let us know what's next," said Todd.

"The next step would be another test. This one is called an Auditory Brainstem Response Test—ABR." Dr. Blackwood reached for a nearby pamphlet and handed it to Todd, who opened it and ran his eyes down the page. My heart began to race.

"For this test," Dr. Blackwood continued, "Conner will be sedated. Once he is fully under, electrodes are placed on his head to measure the brain's reaction to various sounds. It's similar to what we did today, but with the electrodes in place, nothing will be left up to interpretation. This test will give us concrete answers to exactly how extensive Conner's hearing loss is."

"Okay, we'll do that," I said with a nod.

"Yes, please give us a referral as soon as possible," Todd said, his brow scrunched. "We need to know what's going on."

Once we got home, Todd jumped into action, trying to get us an appointment for a sedation test as soon as humanly possible. He first called the place Dr. Blackwood had recommended. It was a six-month wait. He searched for other options and called every number he found, one-by-one. Each place had a waiting list of varying lengths, so he made appointments at all three of them. The shortest waiting period was six weeks. I felt sick.

Time crawled by as Todd called around each day to check for last-minute openings. Meanwhile, I tried to go through the motions of everyday life, caring for Conner while toggling between bright, sunny hopefulness and utter despair. In my brighter moments, I'd giggle as Conner laughed hysterically each time I kissed his round belly, smiled big, and said, "*Ahhhh*, BOOP!"

In those moments, life felt sweet and airy, like all of our worries were for nothing. He could hear me—he had to hear me! Otherwise he wouldn't be laughing so hard! Plus, even if he did have a bit of hearing loss, it wouldn't be a big deal; it'd just be something unique about him, like his sweet doughy legs and big gummy smile.

Sadly, the bright outlook never lasted long. As quickly as it came, it would disappear beneath the weight of *what ifs* that sprinted through my mind. In those moments, I'd find a way to get Conner settled as quickly as possible so I could try to regain my bearings. It was impossible not to let my mind wander to the most terrible places. Had Conner never heard my voice? Had he never heard me say *I love you*? Had he never heard the classical music I played, Todd's silly dad jokes, or the simple creaks and tip-taps of our beloved home?

I spent countless hours studying, obsessing, and poring over research about infant hearing loss. In every study I read, the signs matched perfectly what we were seeing in Conner—or did they? He was so little, it was impossible to tell what was real and what was imagined. I moved on to researching the ABR test and what to expect, which led me to research on sedation in infants and horror story after horror story. I thought back to Dr. Riley and how flippant he was, how he seemed to think there was no reason to pursue answers. It made me grit my teeth and look past my fears about the anesthesia. If something was really wrong, Conner deserved for us to know. Only then could we intervene.

In all this, Todd put every ounce of energy he had into searching for anyone who had any connections at medical practices that dealt with hearing loss. Desperate to get us in somewhere sooner, he made countless calls and pursued every lead he could unearth. Together, we went down every inroad we could; it was our way of seeking control in a situation where we had absolutely none. In the end, we were forced to wait the full six weeks, toggling back and forth between anxiety and acceptance and back again. We lived each day in survival mode.

As the day of the test approached, Todd and I were bleary-eyed and ready for answers. Because of the sedation, Conner wasn't allowed to nurse at all past midnight. He was still a ravenous, growing boy, so he spent the night inconsolable, his wails so sharp and pointed they cut the air like machetes through overgrown brush. I did my best to comfort him with a pacifier, holding him close to my chest and bouncing him as I nodded in and out of sleep.

"Come on, buddy," I whispered. "It's gonna be okay."

When we got ourselves dressed and out the door, the sun was just beginning to peek above the horizon. I sat in the backseat, my hand holding the pacifier in Conner's mouth as he fell into restless sleep, his brows scrunched and fists balled. Anytime we hit a small bump, he woke up and started screaming again. My motherly instinct was on overdrive, compelling me to reach into his seat, pull him out, and let him latch. My heart hammered the inside of my chest as I leaned into him, whispering, "*Shhhh, shhhh, shhhh.*"

Forty-five minutes later, we pulled into the parking lot and rushed into the hospital. We sat in the waiting room, in stiff chairs and surrounded by stained children's books and out-of-date parenting magazines, and I bounced Conner on my lap as he kept screaming. Todd placed his hand on my back, his lips pressed together. He leaned in to Conner.

"It's okay, buddy," he said. "This'll all be over soon."

The door opened with a metallic *groan*, and a nurse in pink scrubs stepped out.

"Conner McKittrick?" she asked. Todd and I stood clumsily, gathering our things as Conner's breath hitched. "Follow me this way—second door to the right."

We walked into the examination room and placed our things on two plastic chairs in the corner. I stared at the hospital bed with its railings pulled up. I wanted to take Conner and run. Instead, I swallowed the lump forming in my throat.

"All right, Mom and Dad," the nurse said. "If you'll just get Conner undressed, into a clean, dry diaper, and put him in this gown, we'll be all set."

"How long will this take?" I asked.

"Conner is our first patient today, and the test shouldn't be more than thirty minutes to an hour." She patted the tiny hospital gown on the plastic mattress. "Once he's all set in this, we can begin."

As soon as the nurse left the room, I began fumbling with Conner's clothes. My hands shook as I unsnapped his onesie and wrestled him out of it, turning my back to block Todd from coming over to help. I felt as though I might lose it if anyone tried to touch Conner but me. I slipped the ugly gown over his head, snapped it closed as best I could, then brought him to my chest. My heart leapt as I heard a *knock, knock* and the door opened. The nurse re-entered room, the anesthesiologist by her side. He was a tall, bald man in blue scrubs and a cap.

"Hi there," he said. "I'm Doctor Alan."

"Hi," I managed.

"Good morning," Todd said.

"All right, I know we don't want to drag this out. I see our little boy is having a tough time." Conner sniffed. "Right now, let's get him situated on the bed. If you'll stick with him, Mom, I'm going to place this mask over his nose and mouth and give him some nitrous oxide—just a small dose. This will get him nice and calm so we can take him back and get him sedated."

I knew we wouldn't be allowed back, but my face still flushed pink.

"If you'll just place him on the bed, Mom..." the doctor continued.

I brought Conner to the bed, steeling myself as he clawed at me, trying to get back into my arms. Dr. Alan placed the mask over his nose and mouth as he wiggled and screamed, desperately trying to get away.

One breath...

Then two...

And his body relaxed. I carefully took my hand out from beneath his head and kissed his plump cheek, the rough edge of the mask grazing my lips. Todd came over and ran his hand along Conner's hairline.

"We'll be right here waiting," he whispered.

"If you'll just head back out to the waiting room," the nurse said as she began to maneuver the bed out of its space by the wall, "we'll come grab you when we're all done." Two other nurses entered the room and helped guide the bed through the door with a *clank, clank.*

Todd and I made our way back out into the waiting room, where images of Conner limp in the bed, his head covered in electrodes, made my stomach turn. I watched as people filtered in and out, some with anguished looks on their faces, some calm and serene. I couldn't do anything but sit and stare at the floor below me, my tired eyes tracing cracks in the well-worn tile. I already had a huge fear of hospitals, and I especially hated that Conner had to be in one.

An hour later, we were called back in. Conner was lying in the bed, still in the rumpled hospital gown, his eyes open but droopy. I rushed to his side and scooped him up, immediately taking him to the chair in the corner and letting him latch. I winced as he fed; he was so hungry that his jaw pulsed as he took quick gulps, letting out short sniffs and long sighs. Todd sat in the chair beside me, his hand on my knee. The nurse's shoe squeaked as she walked into the room.

"Conner did great," she said. I nodded. "As soon as you finish up, you'll follow me out to the doctor's office."

I quickly switched Conner to the other side, let him drain all of the milk my body had produced, and quickly gathered up our things. Todd and I followed the nurse down the hall into a sterile office with nothing on the walls. Todd bounced his knee and I tapped my foot as we waited, jumping at every small sound that came from the hallway. Finally, the doctor came through the door, a thick file folder in her hands.

"Mr. and Mrs. McKittrick, so nice to meet you. I'm Sharon, the audiologist," she said, shaking each of our hands. "I have Conner's results right here."

She opened the file and shuffled the papers, pulling one out and flipping it around so we could see it.

"This is what we call an audiogram," she said. "Have you seen one of these before?"

"Sort of—when we did the booth test," I said, leaning in closer.

"All right, let me explain. As you know, the Auditory Brainstem Response test exists to gauge the patient's ability to hear at all volume levels. The vertical lines on this report represent pitch or frequency; the horizontal lines represent loudness or intensity. On the pitch or frequency side, we're looking very closely at the 500-4,000 hertz levels, since that is where normal speech falls. The quietest sound the patient can hear is recorded in this report—we call the resulting line a 'speech banana.' On this report, the x's represent the left ear, and the o's represent the right. The pictures here represent different sounds we hear every day—an airplane, a dog barking, et cetera."

"So, how did he do?" Todd asked.

"To understand this, I need to explain that there are varying levels of deafness," the audiologist replied. "The scale goes from mild to moderate to severe hearing loss, all the way to profound deafness." She drew a breath, and my stomach flipped. "Mr. and Mrs. McKittrick, Conner's test has revealed that he is profoundly deaf."

My breath caught—all I heard was the word "deaf" and my heart began slamming against the walls of my chest. Molten hot tears stung my eyes. I patted Conner's back, then kissed him over and over again on the head.

"What does this mean?" Todd asked.

Dr. Sharon rustled some papers, worked one out of the pile, and slid it our way. On it were pictures of children with hearing aids on, round discs fastened to the sides of their heads.

"There is some good news," she continued. "I believe Conner will be an excellent candidate for cochlear implants."

"Wh-what is that?" Todd asked.

"These are devices that stimulate the auditory nerve through electrodes placed on the cochlea, in the inner ear. Stimulating it can allow profoundly deaf individuals to perceive sound. However, there is the cost to consider. These start at $30,000, and in most cases, they are not covered by insurance."

"Whatever the cost, we'll make it work," Todd said, taking the paper. I rubbed my eyes and kissed Conner on the head again.

"I know this isn't the result you were hoping for," Dr. Sharon said, her lips curled into a sympathetic smile. "I need you to know: there is hope for Conner. He will lead a full, happy life."

We gathered our things and moved silently through the hallway, down the elevator, and out into the frigid Washington winter. I placed Conner in his car seat and buckled him in, fighting tears. The thought of Conner having to navigate deafness swirled into the dreadful idea of needing to sell our house or take out a massive loan to afford cochlear implants. As soon as Todd sank into his seat and closed the car door, I couldn't help myself—the words poured from my mouth.

"What the heck are we going to do?"

"I don't know," Todd replied, shaking his head.

As Todd navigated the car onto the highway, we processed all of the possible scenarios aloud, desperately wishing for answers where there seemed to be none. I looked down and stared into Conner's wide eyes. I wanted to tell him how much I loved him, how safe he was, how we wouldn't stop fighting for him. I pressed my lips together before I began to speak.

But it didn't matter what I had to say.

He couldn't hear me anyway.

Three

T HE NEXT DAY, TODD and I sat at the table, bleary-eyed. Neither of us had slept. He sipped a glass of soda, and I drained my cup of coffee. Conner was asleep in his crib, and the house was silent. Todd drew a breath and reached for the stack of papers in the middle of the table. He flipped through them slowly, reading the report again, as if it would somehow reveal different results if he just looked a little harder. I poured some more coffee, took my mug into the other room, and sat in front of our desktop. I punched in search terms as steam from my mug swirled in the lamplight, still hoping that I'd find some hope I hadn't yet uncovered. The computer tower groaned as results popped up on the page—halfway down, I saw a listing that hadn't previously caught my eye. It was for a school called Listen and Talk. I clicked, and my heart began to race as my eyes danced down the page. There, at the very top of their website was their tagline:

No child is limited by hearing loss.

"Todd!" I called.

"What? Did you find something?" He asked, jogging to my side.

"I think so," I said. "Look—it's a school for children with hearing loss.

It's in Seattle. This could be it. Oh my gosh, listen to this." I began to read aloud from the website: "'Our listening and spoken language program graduates enter their neighborhood school by kindergarten and learn and compete side-by-side with hearing peers in regular classrooms. Converse and learn through spoken and written language. Reach their full language and learning potential and fully integrate into the wider community.' Todd, this could help."

I fumbled for the phone and quickly punched in their number, tapping my foot as I listened to the automated menu before pressing three to leave a message.

"Hi there, my name is Lane McKittrick. We received a profound deafness diagnosis for our son, Conner, yesterday. We don't know what to do, we..." I steadied myself. "We'd just really appreciate a call back." I left my number, put the phone down, and took a deep breath.

"This is a good step," Todd said. "We're going to figure this out."

I nodded.

Conner began to cry.

We went through the motions of the afternoon, playing with Conner on the floor, feeding him, and trying to capture some semblance of normalcy. But every meal we ate, every activity we did, every moment of our lives was now tainted with the questions that swirled in our minds:

Will Conner ever hear his own child cry?

Will he ever hear his spouse's voice?
Will he get married at all?
Is his life ruined?
Will he be okay?

As the afternoon faded into evening, I settled in front of a basket brimming with clean laundry. I folded onesies, burp cloths, tiny pairs of pants, and little socks. I felt sick. These chores felt so trivial—so small beneath the weight of everything we were carrying. That's when the phone rang. The caller ID flashed a Seattle number. My stomach filled with butterflies.

"Todd! They're calling!" I said, answering the phone. "This is Lane."

"Lane, it's so great to speak with you! I'm Michelle from Listen and Talk."

"Michelle, I can't believe you'd call on the weekend. This means so much to us."

"Of course. I know those first few days can be tough."

I put the phone on speaker.

"I have my husband, Todd, here with me. Yes, it's been a hard day or so—to be honest, we're really freaking out."

"I understand," Michelle said, her voice firm but warm and reassuring. "I know that it can be hard to find resources about hearing loss and deafness, but please know, I'm here to help. Please, give me all of your questions."

Todd and I sat on the phone with Michelle for more than two hours, asking her every single question we'd been mulling over. She patiently and methodically answered each one. We learned that Listen and Talk provided everything we were looking for: answers, guidance, assistance, *community*. She went on to give us all the resources we needed for hearing aids, cochlear implants, and more. The school itself had auditory-verbal therapy along with a full program that ran from infancy through preschool. Michelle let us know that we would qualify for disability programs through the state, and, as a first step, we had to contact Family Services so they could assess Conner. That test would allow them to put together an Individualized Family Services Plan (IFSP). These would finally be our first steps to getting Conner the help he needed—outside of the implants, which we'd continue to pursue on our own. Michelle even offered to coordinate with us to help us get a case manager she'd worked with in the past.

By the time our call drew to a close, Todd and I were feeling some semblance of hope. At the very least, we now knew there were people out there who were ready and willing to help.

"I can't thank you enough," I said, suddenly noticing that my shoulders had relaxed.

"Of course," Michelle replied. "I'll get the IFSP meeting all set up. And, please: keep in touch. We'd love to have you come down to the school as things start to settle."

With several pages of scribbled notes in-hand, we ended the call. Low light was filtering through the kitchen window, a sure sign that night was about to fall. This time, however, the looming darkness didn't feel so bleak.

Although the hospital where we'd done the Auditory Brainstem Response test was able to offer us a few inroads into cochlear implants, specifically the number of an organization we could call about hearing aids for children, there was nothing beyond that—no information about our communication options for Conner and very little else to go on. With very little direction, we desperately started searching for hospitals that did implants and quickly learned that there were very few—only three in Washington State—and that none of them could implant kids as young as Conner due to FDA regulations. But we didn't care. We wanted to get in to see a doctor as soon as possible so we could get some answers.

We ignored the age restrictions and made appointments at the two hospitals that did implants in toddlers. Of course, the waiting lists were months long, so Todd set about calling each hospital every day, hoping something would open sooner. On top of that, Todd began doggedly pursuing appointments at clinics around town, doing everything he could to get us in somewhere that might be able to do something to help. We spent hours poring over our finances, trying to figure out how we would even afford implants if we could get them. Ultimately, we decided it didn't matter—we'd try to get insurance to pay, and if they wouldn't, we'd set up some kind of a payment plan.

In all this, I did my best to focus on Conner, and on keeping him as happy as humanly possible. We knew that one of our first steps toward implants was attempting hearing aids, which we were required to do before Conner could be considered as a candidate for cochlear implants. We coordinated with a rental company to get the hearing aids, which were cumbersome and difficult to put on. Still, I had Conner's ears fitted and did my best to try them out with him. I was fumbling my way through caring for him now that I knew he was profoundly deaf, making things up as I went. I still spoke to him the same way, making the same big faces and the same loud noises, and he still giggled and wiggled, showing me his big, toothless smile. My heart ached as I went through the motions of motherhood, still plagued by stabbing questions about all the things his future held.

One week later, the day of our IFSP meeting arrived. I hustled around the kitchen in the morning light, gathering mugs while a pot of coffee brewed. This was our chance to determine our family's needs: the team would decide what support was necessary and put the appropriate systems in place. I bounced Conner on my hip as Todd did the last of the straightening up.

Knock, knock.

Todd rushed to the door as I made my way out to the living room. A gust of cold air swept through the house as Michelle walked in with a tall, slight woman with short brown hair—our new case manager. My mouth burst into a smile as I locked eyes with Michelle. I'm not a hugger, but I couldn't help myself from putting my arms around her.

"I'm so happy to see you," I said, gripping her.

"Same to you—hello, Conner!" She said with a big wave, grabbing his toes.

Conner giggled.

"Hi there, I'm Ellen," the case manager said, sticking out her hand. "Thank you so much for welcoming me into your home."

Together, we all walked into the living room and each took a seat. I sat on the floor with Conner in my lap, holding him beneath his arms as he kicked at the floor. Ellen cleared her throat.

"All right, let's quickly go over some goals for the meeting so that we're all on the same page," she began. "As you all know, Conner, because of his recent hearing test results, qualifies for an IFSP. So, we are here to create an IFSP for your family. That way, we can get the ball rolling on services, therapies, education, and so on."

I nodded.

"To do that," she continued, "let's get started by talking through our goals. I know Michelle well, and have worked with Listen and Talk for many years, so I think I understand the communication model you've chosen. I see here that you'll be pursuing cochlear implants?"

"That's right," Todd said. "I'm working on getting us in somewhere as soon as possible."

"Fantastic," Ellen replied. "I know the wait can be long, but we'll get services in place in the meantime, all right? It's good that you've gotten him fitted for hearing aids."

For the next several hours, we sat together in the dappled sunlight talking about Conner, our hopes for him, and all the ways we ideally wanted to be supported. Ellen went back over the results of the ABR test, and asked us a lot of questions. By the time the meeting drew to a close, Todd and I locked eyes and smiled at one another. Michelle and Ellen left the house with promises to follow up later in the week, and I stood in the doorway with Conner, wiggling his hand in a stiff wave as we watched them drive away.

Four

T ODD AND I SAT side-by-side, a Diet Pepsi in the cupholder between our seats. My throat was tight, my shoulders tense. Earlier that day, I'd come across a listing for a movie that had just won several awards at the Seattle Film Festival. The film was called *Sound and Fury*. I could hardly believe it: it was about Deaf two cousins and their families navigating all the challenges that came with their diagnoses—it was the first time I'd ever seen Deafness spelled with a capital *D*! I'd frantically searched for showtimes and found it playing at a small independent movie theater nearby as part of a local film festival. I hurriedly called my mom, arranged for her to come stay with Conner, and told Todd to get ready.

I was glad we'd come to see the movie, but in the darkness, I found my heart racing. The topic of cochlear implants came up as the family wrestled with the idea of getting them. The parents feared that the implants would impact the children's relationship with Deaf culture. Todd and I left the theater in a daze, new questions percolating in our minds.

Were we making a mistake by pursuing implants?

Should we be going back to the drawing board and weighing our options?

The audiologist who diagnosed Conner never even mentioned other communication models. That seemed wrong, yet we both came to the same conclusion: if we could, we still wanted Conner to be able to hear like we could. If he wanted to change his mind once he got older, at least we would have given him the opportunity. For now, we needed to find a way to get him those implants, and soon.

Thankfully, it took barely a week for us to get our IFSP from Ellen, and we were grateful to find that our services would be covered through Listen and Talk. I chatted with Michelle and carefully reviewed the programs she suggested. We knew we'd take advantage of all of them, and the very first one was a Parent-Infant/Toddler group at the school.

When the day of our first group arrived, I put Conner in my favorite outfit of his and traded my usual leggings for jeans. I hoisted him out of his car seat and onto my hip and made my way into the building, which smelled like fresh crayons and juice.

The receptionist welcomed us with a big smile and exaggerated hand gestures, greeting Conner with happy waves. We made our way into the room where the play group was being held, and where children played on gym mats with foam blocks, each with a therapist by their side to guide them. I walked over to a chair against the wall, placed my bag on the floor, and sat. A girl in a Listen and Talk T-shirt walked over to me and smiled.

"Who do we have here?" she asked.

"This is Conner," I said. "It's our first day."

"Well, welcome Conner," she said. "Mom, you get settled. May I take Conner to play?"

I nodded, handing Conner over to her.

He let out a soft cry.

The girl rested Conner on her hip and bounced expertly, patting his back. I looked to my left to see three other moms in nearby chairs, leaning forward and watching intently as their toddlers played with therapists nearby. One of them looked over to me.

"How old is your son?" she said.

"He's just about to be eight months. How old is yours?"

"Mine is almost nineteen months—her son is seventeen months," she said, gesturing to the woman next to her, who waved at me.

"I'm Jenny," she said.

"I'm Lane," I replied, waving back.

"I'm Amanda," the first woman said. "Your son is adorable. Is this your first day?" I nodded.

"We were only diagnosed a couple of weeks ago."

"Gosh, I remember that time," Jenny said, shaking her head. "So, so hard. Are you holding up okay?"

"Some days yes, some days no." I chewed the inside of my cheeks; it was the first time I'd answered that question honestly.

"We've both been there," Amanda said. "It took me a while to find this place, but it's been a complete game changer."

I glanced down at Jenny's son. He was playing on a nearby mat, laughing and tumbling, his light brown cochlear implant resting on either side of his head, of seemingly little consequence to him.

"I see your son has a cochlear implant," I said. "Has he done well with it?"

"Insanely well," she replied. "He just got it a few months ago. It's a long, bumpy process, but it's really so worth it."

"We're going that route too," I replied, picking at my nails. "But it's been hard."

"Calling everywhere, trying to get in?"

"Yes. I can't believe the wait."

"I know, it's awful."

"*Of course,* Conner isn't technically old enough, but we want to get them taken care of as soon as we can. We just want him to live a normal life."

"I know," Amanda added, nodding. "You just have to be patient. Seriously, you'll get through it and you'll have a surgery date soon. You just can't let up."

For the entire hour Conner played with his therapist and interacted with other children, I dissected every moment of my experience with Amanda and Jenny. The conversation was peppered with too many *me too's* and *same here's* to count. After so many weeks of trying to explain what was going on to friends and family, it felt incredible to talk to two people who really understood exactly what we were going through. As our family hurdled towards our next steps, this was exactly what we so desperately needed: connection.

As the weeks wore on, Todd continued to push to get Conner in for a cochlear implant appointment as soon as possible. When the phone rang or while he was waiting on hold, thoughts of the procedure, therapies, and recovery would start to creep into our heads, only interrupted by when a receptionist finally answered and brought us back to reality. The sheer volume of information paired with all the emotions around the implant process was invading our collective minds. On top of invasive surgery and a lifetime of therapy and learning, we were still in for, to put it mildly, an uphill battle—*forever*. It felt like we were rushing into a fire.

In the meantime, I was solely focused on Conner and his care. Our entire lives had become about putting our IFSP plan into place and working the Listen and Talk program. There was the Parent-Infant/Toddler group at the school, occupational therapy somewhere else, auditory-verbal therapy at the house, and more. Soon, we were spending more time with therapists than we were with friends or family. As much work as it was to get ourselves to all of the appointments, we knew they were all necessary and would go a long way toward making us feel like we were doing right by Conner.

During the home sessions, I sat on the floor beside the therapist who taught me everything I needed to know about communicating with Conner. The first thing I learned were the six "ling" sounds, which are the easiest for people to hear—*ah, ee, oo, sh, s,* and *mm*. My whole life came to revolve about those sounds. They'd guide me through propping Conner up in front of me, saying things like, "The COW goes MMMMMMMMOOOOOOOOO!" and "The AIRPLANE goes AAAAAAAAHHHH!" We had toys that we'd lift in front of him that corresponded to each of the spoken sounds, and soon, the floor was littered with piles of plastic cats, cows, airplanes, trucks, and cars. Every time we ate, with each bite, I'd exclaim, "MMMM, YUM, YUM!"

We learned to narrate everything to him. I loved every minute of it, because I hoped it would make a difference—but it was exhausting.

Regardless of how much work we put in, Conner wasn't making much progress. In fact, though things were changing, he was becoming more volatile. Unable to communicate any of his needs, he was beginning to get frustrated more easily. He would sob and his breath would hitch as I tried to guess what he needed: A diaper? A snack? A drink of milk? A hug? My life had become a constant stream of trial and error as I tried to meet the needs of a growing boy who was desperate to communicate. Although I'm not someone who cries readily or often, I'd often find myself standing over him exhausted, tears streaming down my face. I was there for my baby boy and ready to give him the world, but without any way to communicate, I was left with only his blood curdling screams and a broken heart.

Often inconsolable, Conner soon began to refuse to breastfeed, which demolished me. I'd pick him up as he screamed, his face so red it was nearly purple, and bring him to my breast. He'd flail and shriek, pushing away from me with all his might. Those quiet moments when he latched on and nuzzled into me, softly snorting as he gulped, were gone, and I was grieving. I wasn't ready to let go of that connection, but I couldn't force him to nurse. I wistfully transitioned him to bottles, saying goodbye to a cornerstone of our beautiful bond.

Though much of Conner's screaming was hard to decode, we knew one thing for sure: He was still dealing with excruciating ear infections so intense that he'd spend days on end shrieking and clawing at his head. After Dr. Riley pushed off our concerns about Conner's hearing, we began looking for new doctors, which proved difficult after Conner's diagnosis. His file was now two inches thick, and we couldn't get a doctor to actually read it (or even skim it) before an appointment. When you're only allotted twenty minutes of a doctor's time, it's impossible to explain everything, so I finally resigned myself to waving and saying, "Yes, he's deaf. We're doing speech therapy and pursuing cochlear implants. We've got it all handled." But inside, I couldn't help but wonder why I felt so alone. If we didn't help Conner, who would?

While we waited for our implant appointment, Conner once again started screaming and pulling at his ears. I quickly sprang into action, going about the routine of getting him in with a doctor right away. This time, we were scheduled with a new doctor at the same practice we were trying out. She was young—just out of med school—and shook her head as she stuck the orthoscope into his ears one by one.

"Good news, Mom—it's not an ear infection," she said.

"I think you should look again," I replied as Conner shuddered.

"I don't need to; I don't see any cause for concern."

"Please, just check once more," I begged. "He's been screaming like he does when he has an infection. We need to get him on medication."

She placed the orthoscope in both ears again and, after a moment, shook her head.

"I understand that he gets them a lot, but he doesn't have one now," she replied. "Just keep him comfortable with Tylenol."

I knew she was wrong, but there was nothing I could do. I took him home, gave him Tylenol, and put him into his pajamas. That night, Todd and I bounced him as he cried out, clawing at his ears as if he wanted to rip them off. Around midnight, he let out the most intense, sharp scream I'd ever heard. My eyes were like saucers as I squinted at his right ear; there was clear fluid leaking out of it. We gathered him up and rushed to the emergency room where a doctor checked his ears beneath yellow, halogen lights.

"His right eardrum—it burst," he said. "The result of a nasty infection. You really should have had him checked out when symptoms first appeared."

"We did," I managed.

"Well," he said, walking to the sink, "sometimes doctors make mistakes."

I STARED AT CONNER as he lay beneath a thin white sheet, his eyes fluttering softly. Todd placed his hand on my knee and squeezed. I smiled at him, pressing my lips together. Although we had become familiar with the process of having Conner sedated, it never got any easier. As soon as we walked into the hospital, Conner would start to fuss. Todd would head to reception to get us checked in as Conner's anxiety kicked in. As I bounced him, my heart would race knowing that he was about to be poked and prodded by doctors. I knew what we were doing was ultimately good for Conner, but my stomach tied itself in knots as I imagined gloved hands, needles, and swirls of tubes. Of course, then came the nurses and doctors with the saccharine smiles, going through the motions, calling me "Mom," which always felt rehearsed. It never failed that once I'd undressed Conner and placed him in an ugly, stiff hospital gown, the sight of a mask being placed over his nose and mouth made me want to punch the anesthesiologist, gather Conner in my arms, and run.

I kept staring at Conner, picking at my nails while willing him to wake up. Although having him sedated was awful, we were fortunate that, this time, we were going to be able to take care of two things while he was under.

First, the doctor would place tubes in Conner's ears to stop the constant ear infections. Having endlessly researched the procedure, I learned that, although common, the surgery wasn't exactly *simple*. A hole had to be cut into the eardrum to facilitate the tube, which would then release the fluid from the ear so it didn't sit there and cause an infection. Cutting into an eardrum seemed almost cruel for someone who couldn't use them, but keeping Conner's ear canal free and clear of recurring infections would keep us out of the pediatrician's office. It would also make it far more likely that we could get through the cochlear implant surgery smoothly; after all, the doctors wouldn't operate on Conner if he had an active infection at the time of surgery, so we couldn't risk it.

Second, since an additional ABR hearing test was a necessary part of the journey toward cochlear implants, we could have that test done while he was sedated as well. Of course, Todd and I knew what the results would be before the audiologist came to talk to us: as expected, it was confirmed that Conner was profoundly deaf.

I stood and crossed the room as Conner stirred. I reached into the bed, placed my hands under him, and scooped him up, kissing him all over his face. He blinked his eyes and nuzzled into my shoulder, letting out a tired sigh. Just as Conner settled in, a sharp pain shot through my chest. I moved Conner to my hip, adjusted my grip, and carefully pressed the heel of my hand into the side of my right breast. The pain was instant, and as I moved my hand, I realized how firm the tissue was. I had to admit that I'd noticed my breasts were swollen that morning, but I'd been rushing around and didn't stop to fully take note. Now, beneath the halogen lights of the doctor's office, I was paying attention.

In the weeks prior, Todd and I had openly discussed trying for another baby. Yes, part of me felt like it was an insane choice to make with everything going on, but we'd fallen into a steady rhythm with Conner's care. Our life had become a well-choreographed dance; we each had our own parts, and we played them exceedingly well. Life was busy and chaotic, but that was what it meant to be a parent. We loved Conner with every ounce of our being and simply accepted the work we were doing on his behalf as an extension of that love. Since we wanted a big family, we figured there was no better time to try than now.

I ran my hands over Conner's hair and smiled softly. Todd walked over with a smile and placed his hand on Conner's back.

"Hey, buddy," he said. "How was your nap?"

"Todd," I said, resting my hand on his forearm. "I think I'm pregnant."

His face lit up.

"I know," I said. "Let's get a pregnancy test on the way home."

We got Conner dressed, checked out, and got into our car. Before we got home, we stopped at a pharmacy near our house and grabbed a test. Within the hour, we were in the bathroom clutching the test wrapped in toilet paper and waiting for the results. Finally, I looked down in disbelief and then at Todd.

"We're pregnant!" I exclaimed.

Todd wrapped his arms around me.

"I can't believe we get to do this all again," he said. "Big family, here we come! I love you so much, Lane."

"I love you too."

I curled up on the bed next to Todd. In that moment, the stress of the day seemed like a distant memory. All I could do was look to the future and smile widely at the thought of Conner having a sibling to share his life with. I could already see them nestled on the carpet, together playing with cars and toy airplanes, and sharing belly laughs and big smiles as they shouted, "The airplane goes AAAAHHHHHHH!"

"Happy birthday to you! Happy birthday to you! Happy birthday, dear Conner! Happy birthday to you!" friends and family sang in unison.

"Make a wish!" I said, leaning forward as Conner bounced excitedly in his high chair. He blew a raspberry as I took the reins and blew out the flames. The small crowd cheered as smoke danced around the extinguished candles. I picked up the cake and brought it to a nearby table, cutting it into chunks and placing them on blue paper plates.

"Let me help," my mom said, nudging me aside.

"Thanks," I replied, wiping my hands on a napkin and glancing around. My eyes flitted from face to face, and I couldn't help but smile. Looking back at the past year, I couldn't believe all we'd been through: the discovery of Conner's deafness, those terrifying first appointments, the IFSP, the constant work to keep Conner and our family headed toward a "normal" life. As I watched our friends and family mingle, digging into big wedges of cake with green frosting, all I felt was love—and, now, our family was growing.

I was in the throes of battling the dreaded exhaustion that comes with early pregnancy— bone-tired, but with no time to indulge my desire to rest. I'd recently gone back to work, so life had become extremely full. I'd get up and get myself ready, then, usually, Todd would take Conner to daycare. I'd take the bus to work, get through my day poring over paperwork and spearheading meetings, and then take the bus home to transition into full Mom mode. As soon as I tossed my bag aside and changed Conner's diaper, I'd get down onto the floor and begin the usual series: "The airplane goes AAAAAAHHHHHHHH!" and "The cow goes MOOOOOO!" until it was time for dinner, swiftly followed by Conner's bath and bedtime.

I handled my intense cravings for watermelon on the go, by chopping up a whole one and tossing it into containers so I could munch at will throughout the day. I was living life on autopilot, all while working toward cochlear implant day, which was swiftly approaching.

Through all of our hard work, constant phone calls, meetings, and appointments with specialists, Todd and I were somehow able to get the approval to implant Conner at fourteen months. He would be the youngest child ever implanted at the hospital, and we were absolutely thrilled. However, that meant we only had two months to squeeze in every required appointment, all while keeping Conner as healthy as possible to avoid having his surgery pushed back or canceled. A friend who lived close by happened to be an ENT and did quick and regular checks on Conner with an otoscope, which became more frequent as we got closer to the date. We were so grateful for the time he was willing to invest in helping us towards the big day. Still, it was proving more difficult than I ever imagined to build a community we could really connect with.

Though I maintained friendships with the moms at Listen & Talk, it was different than having a best friend who could come over in sweatpants and let me spill about the hard stuff. As I moved through all my interactions, I listened to myself as I talked to friends. Over and over, I was downplaying what we were going through. Everyone around us had a rosy image of our lives, as if things were fairly easy and the implant surgery was a miracle on the horizon. Everyone seemed to think we still had the capacity to talk through their small dramas, which actually felt painfully hard to listen to. It was nearly impossible to offer sympathy to someone complaining about a rude mom at school pickup or a kid who was a picky eater when our life sometimes felt like a fractured mess. I had to remind myself constantly that those around me could only operate with the information available to them; I couldn't resent anyone for a lack of understanding or compassion when I wasn't sharing enough to raise their concern. I sometimes wished that I could push past the need to keep it all together, even with the people who loved me most, but I couldn't help it. I didn't want sympathy, syrupy sweet gestures, or worst of all, pity. I preferred to appear happy and strong at all times.

I stared at Conner as he sat in his chair, squishing the cake between his fingers and rubbing it all over his face, leaving streaks of green buttercream. His big smile, with his tiny little front teeth popping out of his pink gums, was perfect. I walked to his side and kissed his head. He giggled as Todd snapped a picture: a moment of pure joy, frozen in time.

Six

I SAT AT THE dining table with the phone pressed against my ear, my eyes tracing swirling knots in the wood.

"I know this isn't what you want to hear the day before your son's surgery," the surgeon on the other end of the line said, "but your insurance company has denied the claim."

My throat tightened.

"I know, Mrs. McKittrick, that this is challenging, but we have options. Why don't we push the surgery back a bit so we have time to file an appeal and—?"

"No, we don't want to push the surgery back," I interrupted. "Is there anything else we can do? We've worked so hard for this. There is no way we're turning back now."

"I understand, and an appeal really is your next step." My cheeks were hot.

"I know, but there's no time left. There has to be *something* you can do. Please, I'm begging you."

"All right, there is one thing I can try: How about I call the company myself and make an informal appeal on your behalf?"

"That would be amazing," I said, rubbing my eyes.

"I'll make the call today," she said. "There are no guarantees, but I will try. With any luck, we'll see you tomorrow." Then, she clicked off the line.

I rubbed my belly as I stared at Conner strapped in his high chair, banging plastic figurines of horses, cows, and goats on his tray. He looked up at me with his face scrunched, and he started to wave his hands and let out soft grunts. I stood up and walked over to him.

"What's wrong, buddy?" I asked.

He kept waving his hands and shaking his head.

"What do you need, Conner?"

He let out a sharp cry.

Then another.

Then another.

Soon, he was screaming at the top of his lungs. I stood up and pulled him from the chair, bouncing softly as I rested him on my hip.

"*Shhhh...*" I whispered.

As I pulled him into me, he began to kick and wail, yanking at my hair and shaking his head violently. I checked his diaper; it was clean. I put Cheerios in a cup and handed them to him, and he threw them on the floor. I poured him milk. He screamed even louder. After several minutes, I finally placed him on the floor, propped up on a pillow. When I did, he stopped screaming, his breath still hitching as he calmed himself down. I bit my lip and let out a heavy exhale. This was the exact reason we couldn't delay any longer: Conner's frustrations about communication were agonizing. We knew from our time with doctors and therapists that the sooner you could get a child hearing, the better. That way, they could begin to develop the language they needed to communicate. Conner deserved for us to fight for him, and we would— come hell or high water.

By the time the sun rose the next day, we still hadn't heard back from the insurance company. After speaking to the surgeon, Todd and I had resigned ourselves to the fact that we'd need to pay for the implant out of pocket. We dialed the financial counselor at the hospital, and thankfully, we were able to expedite a payment plan: We'd pay the $30,000 over thirty-six months, interest free. Although it was a big stretch for us, we didn't care. We knew this was Conner's best chance at a future where he could thrive.

The sky was a dusty rose as I strapped Conner into his car seat and buckled myself beside him. Unable to eat for twelve hours prior to the anesthesia, Conner was starving, wailing anytime his pacifier came out of his mouth and rolling to the floor. My belly flip-flopped as Todd navigated the winding roads to the hospital. This would be the longest surgery Conner had ever had—four hours while the surgeon placed the internal part of the device. I knew that if I focused too hard on the procedure itself, I'd make myself sick, so I tried to focus on what was to come. Conner would get to hear my voice for the first time, and soon.

When we got to the hospital, it was business as usual. We wrestled Conner out of his car seat and brought him inside. The sterile smell of rubbing alcohol and latex swirled around me as we checked in and sat down on well-worn chairs. Though our insurance company wasn't helping us at all, the hospital staff did everything they could to work things out to save us as much money as possible. The surgeon even went so far as to push the surgery back a few hours to let us try one last time with the insurance company, but we couldn't get it sorted—then, the otolaryngologist spoke with the anesthesiologist and asked him to work with Conner pro bono. The staff also agreed to let us go home that day rather than spending the night, as long as Conner wasn't showing any signs of infection.

As we waited in the waiting room, I squeezed Conner's little hands and took deep breaths to prepare for what was to come. Eventually, a petite nurse in purple scrubs called us back, and we headed to an examination room to be asked all the usual questions. I juggled Conner as I undressed him, changed his diaper, and pulled the gown over his head. I took him in my arms and held him against my chest until the anesthesiologist came in and asked me to place Conner on the bed. He eased the mask over Conner's face as he kicked and screamed. I tightened my jaw as Conner stopped flailing and his eyes drifted shut.

"Mom and Dad, you can head back out to the waiting area now," the nurse said, lifting the rails on the sides of his bed. "I'll be out to get you just as soon as the procedure is complete."

As always, Todd and I gathered our things and made our way into the waiting room, where we went through the motions of trying to keep ourselves busy. We tried to talk about the new baby and how excited we were, but we couldn't without finding our way back to the topic of Conner. We tried playing cards, but we couldn't focus. Eventually, we found ourselves sitting and staring straight ahead. My mind raced.

Are we doing the right thing?

We have to be, right?

We've been through all the consultations and understand that we should do this.

We should take advantage of the available technology... right?

I mean, if a prosthetic arm or leg can help someone, how is this any different?

What are we doing?

Our baby is in there with someone making tiny holes in his head.

No—don't think that.

He's fine.

I want to go in there.

No—I can't.

He will get through this, and so will I.

He's a strong boy.

I can be strong, too. For him.

Four hours later, my brain felt like it had been through a blender. My eyes were red, hands clammy, and my nails were bitten down to the cuticles. Finally, the door opened with a labored groan. The surgeon came through the door, surgical cap still on her head and a mask hanging over one of her shoulders.

"Mr. and Mrs. McKittrick, the surgery went extremely well," she said. "We were able to place the implant without difficulty, and Conner is recovering as we speak. You're welcome to come back with me now and sit with him while the sedation wears off."

My body relaxed.

My heart rate slowed.

"I'm so glad," Todd replied, blinking back tears.

"Yes, we're so relieved," I added.

"He really did well," the surgeon said with a nod. "I know this has been hard, but we've taken a huge step today. He couldn't have done better. Come on back now, follow me."

We followed the surgeon down the hall to the very last room on the right. My breath caught as we walked through the door and my eyes landed on my baby boy lying there. His eyes were closed, his cheeks sallow and squished. There was a plastic dome over his right ear, covering the incision. Gauze bandages were wrapped around his entire head, pushing his mouth into a pucker. I swallowed hard. A nurse walked in behind us rubbing sanitizer between her hands.

"Mom," she said softly, "you can go ahead and pick him up."

I rushed over to the bed and scooped up Conner as carefully as I could. I tried to rest him against me, gently working around the bandages, wires, and tubes coming out of him. His arms were stiff, fitted into splints that would prevent him from pulling out his IV. I awkwardly tried to find a position to cradle him in. Once I did, I kissed his forehead and met Todd's eyes, which were narrow and glassy.

"I'm glad the surgery is over," he said, running his hand over Conner's head.

"Me too," I managed.

We stayed in that room for several hours, waiting for the anesthesia to wear off. I'd jump every time Conner's eyes flickered, but he remained unconscious for what felt like forever. A steady stream of nurses came in and out to change his bandages and remove tubes, splints, and IVs, one by one. The bandage over his right ear reminded me of a Princess Leia bun. It was so big compared to my little boy that it frightened me, but I didn't let it show in my expression when, finally, Conner's eyes opened at half-mast.

He let out a cry. His tiny arms reached up and wrapped around my chest, holding me in a vice grip as if he were scared I'd leave him in the hands of doctors again. I let myself feel his heart beating against mine and allowed gratitude to overshadow any lingering anxiety I had. He was okay, and soon, he'd be able to hear my voice. Finally, as night fell and a fingernail moon hung itself in the sky, we gathered our things and headed home.

With the implant in place, we now had to wait four weeks before the doctor would activate the device. For a couple of days, this meant navigating life with cumbersome bandages wrapped around a fiery ball of energy. Of course, the bandages would become rumpled or loose, and I'd re-wrap them as best I could. I was relieved when the day came that Todd and I could carefully take them off but scared of what we'd see when we did. I imagined a big slash and a pool of dried blood, a wound that would make me woozy. Instead, beneath the gauze was a small, neat incision behind Conner's ear that looked red but not angry. Todd leaned Conner over the sink and gently washed it with unscented soap, then patted it dry with a clean towel. With the incision cleaned and well on its way to healing, I finally felt able to put the worst of the surgery behind us. All we had to do now was look forward.

Post-surgery, three weeks passed faster than I'd imagined they would. I'd been checking the mail every day, sometimes multiple times, in anticipation of the bill coming from the hospital. I was prepared: the amount would be in the $30,000 range, but we had a plan. Finally, on a chilly Tuesday afternoon, I hopped out of my car after coming home from work with Conner, who I'd gathered from daycare. Balancing my bag and an empty travel coffee mug, I scurried to the mailbox and opened it with a metallic *squeal*, pulling out its wad of envelopes and flipping through them as I made my way back to the house. I cradled the cup in my elbow as I riffled past junk mail and credit card bills—then, I stopped short. My heart raced at what I was holding in my hands. It was the bill from the hospital, and the envelope was thick.

It's okay.

We planned for this.

After jogging back into the house and getting Conner settled, I sat down on the couch, hands clammy. I opened the envelope and pulled out its thick stack of papers. I unfolded it and held it in my hands. *This is it,* I thought.

My eyes scanned the page as I read through expense after expense, some totaling tens of thousands of dollars. It never failed to amaze me how they charged you for every little thing: bandages. Children's Tylenol, bags of saline, tubes. Then, I came to the last page and looked at the very bottom, clenching my teeth as I read the total owed. My heart hammered the walls of my chest and my breath hastened.

Total owed: $35

This has to be a mistake.

I'm reading this wrong.

There's no way.

I took a picture of the bill and sent it to Todd, who was already on his way home. When he walked in the door, he didn't even kiss me hello. Instead, he went straight to the bill and squinted at it.

"This can't be right," he said.

"I know," I replied. "I just can't imagine any scenario where this isn't a mistake. I—"

"You know what?" he interrupted. "Let's just call the hospital and figure this out."

Todd grabbed the phone and called the billing department at the hospital, putting the phone on speaker. It rang four times before a voice at the other end chirped, "Billing, how may I help?"

"Hi, there. This is Todd and Lane McKittrick. Our son underwent cochlear implant surgery there just a few weeks ago. We received the bill today and are just trying to understand it. We were told that insurance wouldn't be covering our son's procedure, but the bill states that our copay is $35. Can you look into that for me?"

"One moment please," she said, placing us on hold. I paced the room as we waited, listening for Conner, who was quietly playing with a pile of toys in his room. I shook my head at Todd.

"This can't be real," I said. "This has to be a mistake." With that, the phone crackled to life.

"Mr. McKittrick? There is no mistake here. It looks like your insurance company did, in fact, cover the procedure. This $35 copay is all you are responsible for.""Hold on," he said. "Are—are you sure?"

"I'm quite certain. Can I help you with anything else?"

"No, thank you, you've been a huge help!" he hung up the phone, beaming. "I can't believe it, Lane! I think the informal appeal worked!"

The relief was palpable, and the joy was overwhelming. Conner would soon be able to hear, but we weren't going to be drowning in debt as a result.

Seven

AS MY BELLY CONTINUED to swell, I found myself constantly reminded that I was missing so much of this pregnancy. Todd and I had been so *go, go, go* all the time that I wasn't taking time to read to the baby, count his kicks, or indulge in a steady stream of sweet treats. Even when we found out we'd be having a boy, we didn't make time to stop and celebrate. We were heads down focused on the *now*, dedicating every moment to making it through.

Todd worked and helped me as much as he could while I remained in survival mode, climbing the ladder at work, hustling Conner to one appointment after another, and keeping our house in order. It wasn't that he wasn't helping; he provided for us financially and had the important role of being the "fun parent." I took a lot of the burden on myself, because I thought no one could do it better than me at the time. I never asked for help, and even though I found myself exhausted most of the time, I tried not to dwell on it. It was all par for the course.

The weeks leading up to activation day were much the same. Some days would crawl by and others would speed by like a freight train; I'd feel beaten up regardless. Finally, when activation day arrived, I could barely contain my excitement. I woke up before the sun and drained two cups of coffee before gently waking Conner and putting him in a pair of jeans and a collared shirt. I wanted him to be a little dressed up for the video we would take, which I knew we'd cherish for a lifetime.

We headed to the car, got ourselves settled, and quickly made our way to the hospital. As I sat next to Conner watching him fiddle with a small stuffed bear, I felt tears welling in my eyes. My son would hear for the first time today, and he didn't even know it. I imagined his face lighting up as he heard my voice for the first time, and the way he'd react with amazement the moment he heard birds singing. The joy I felt—it was nearly too much to contain.

Less than an hour later, I sat with Conner on my lap, bouncing him on my knees. Todd placed his hand on the small of my back as the audiology assistants fiddled with machines and got everything in place. Soon, two assistants pulled up chairs in front of Conner and me and began playing little games with him to keep him engaged. Todd stood up and fiddled with the camcorder, making sure all the settings were just right. There was a soft tap on the door as it opened, and the audiologist strolled through with a smile on her face.

"Conner, it's so good to see you!" she said, tousling his hair and taking a quick look at the incision, which was now a fresh scar. "This looks great—well done, Mom and Dad! Okay, Conner. Ready to get your new equipment turned on?"

"I can't believe today's the day," I said. "It's really happening!"

"I know," Todd added. "The wait has felt so long."

"Yes, I know it's really tough on parents to have to hold tight for weeks following surgery," the audiologist said. "But we're here now, and that's all that matters. Let's get started."

Todd switched the camera on and stood in the corner of the room. The assistants moved over as the audiologist positioned herself in front of Conner, leaned forward, and made sure the magnetic portion of the device was secured properly to the side of Conner's head. She attached the battery pack, handing it to me so I could keep it close by. One of the nurses touched Conner's knee to get him to look at her. As soon as he did, she covered her face.

"AHHHHHHHHH... BOO!" she said, popping out from behind her palms.

"Here we go," the audiologist said, squinting her eyes as she flipped a tiny switch on the battery pack, making a little red light appear on its side. "I'm going to play some soft noises into his cochlear implant. We won't be able to hear them, but they should help him acclimatize to sound."

Conner froze.

His eyes widened.

His hands balled into fists.

He let out a cry—a cry like I have never seen before. His face contorted, terrified by the noise he was hearing.

"AHHHHHHH BOO!" the nurse then said to Conner.

He waited.

He listened.

He let out a wail.

Tears filled my eyes. I didn't know whether to laugh or cry, unable to control the emotions as they rose.

"Conner, it's Mommy," I cried out, scooping him into my arms. "I love you, buddy. I love you, I love you, I love you."

The audiologist rolled her stool over to a computer in the corner and began adjusting knobs. Conner's eyes were wide as she set the volume level—it would remain low to start, then would be raised over a series of follow-ups.

Conner's eyes scrunched as he let out another sharp scream. Todd turned the camera off, wiped a tear from his cheek, and made his way to our side, stooping down.

"Hey, buddy," he said. "I can't believe you can hear me. I love you so much."

"It will take some time for him to adjust," the audiologist said. "In the coming days, plan to work with your therapists and gently ease him into all this. Again, we'll keep the levels low for a few weeks."

I nodded, dabbing my eyes with the heels of my hands. My breath caught as Todd sat down next to me and placed his hand on Conner's chubby arm. As the audiologist tweaked the levels, Conner's eyes darted around the room. He'd kick and wiggle, then stop suddenly and shriek. I held him against my body, watching as a tear dripped from my chin onto his shoulder. I could hardly contain my relief, my joy, my elation. My son had finally heard my voice—and he knew, beyond a shadow of a doubt, how loved he was.

I SAT ON THE floor, my swollen belly resting on my criss-crossed legs. Conner sat across from me, propped up on a plush couch cushion. Between us was the familiar pile of toys—mounds of cows, horses, trains, airplanes, trucks and cars. I picked up a blue car and swooped it in front of Conner as he watched, clutching a duck and a chicken in each hand.

"The car goes BRRR, BEEP BEEP!" I said, my expressions big and animated.

Conner kicked his feet, letting out a, "Gshhhhhh."

"Let's try again! The car goes BRRR, BEEP BEEP!"

This time, he said nothing.

It had been four weeks since the activation, and Conner was adjusting well, despite the fact that the device was cumbersome. The earpiece rested behind his ear, connected to a magnet that fastened to the side of his head where they'd placed the implant. Then, there was the cord attaching the entire thing to a battery pack. The pack was about six inches long and two inches wide, large enough to be difficult to keep attached to a toddler; we were fortunate that one of the women I'd met at Listen & Talk was able to give us a pouch she's designed and sewn herself.

The pouch perfectly fit the battery pack and had straps attached to it, so it could be strapped to Conner's shoulders like a harness, making it easy for him to move freely while he wore it. Even still, the device was finicky. The earpiece would stay in place as long as Conner was still, but the second I got him engaged in play, snack time, or anything at all, it'd come dislodged and fall out, pulling the device off his ear and getting it tangled in the straps, where it would sometimes just dangle. I'd take a deep breath and readjust in those moments, knowing it was still all worth it. My son could hear my voice. He could participate in learning. He finally had a shot at meeting the milestones he'd missed.

"The sheep goes BAAAAAAAAAHH!" I exclaimed.

Conner giggled, but I could tell he was reaching his limit. His cheeks were red, his chin was covered in a small slick of drool, and his hands were balled into fists. I knew we were moments from a meltdown, but I couldn't help but press on. In the past, I'd often give up on working through the Ling sound check to help figure out if he was able to hear all the sounds of speech and Learning to Listen sounds once we reached a certain point: as soon as Conner started to fuss; since I knew Conner couldn't hear anyway at the time, it felt like a bit of a fool's errand. Now, however, it felt like we needed to make up for lost time.

Conner was still woefully behind for his age. He was sitting up and managed to get from one place to another by clumsily crawling or rolling, but he was not yet pulling up much less walking. That worried me to no end, since I'd read that the cochlear implant surgery could further delay mobility. Conner's communication skills were also so limited that he frequently got frustrated and threw massive, earth-shattering tantrums. The situation wasn't sustainable. Now was the time to get him caught up as quickly as we could.

Todd and I were dedicated to using an auditory-verbal model as opposed to American Sign Language (ASL). We were told that adding ASL to the mix would confuse Conner, thus delaying speech even further. All of this was tricky, especially since Todd and my careers were taking off, and we were darting from place to place. We were grateful that we had a teacher of the deaf coming to the house to make sure we were on the right track with the therapy we did on our own, but the visits were only once a month. We were working the IFSP as best we could, utilizing Listen & Talk for weekly auditory-verbal therapy and doing occupational therapy at a center in Seattle to fill in gaps.

Conner was settled into the program at Listen & Talk, but the commute was killing me. Though Todd and I worked well at splitting tasks between us, the drive to and from school and back again was cutting into our days in a big way. Thankfully, our neighbors offered a solution. They called us over to chat one afternoon, excited to share that they were hiring a nanny, but didn't need her full-time. They asked if we wanted to participate in a nanny share. Our answer was a resounding, "Yes!"

Our nanny quickly became a key player in making everything work. I was also fortunate to be able to adjust my work schedule so I could work longer days Monday through Thursday, allowing me to dedicate all of Friday to Conner's vast array of appointments and trips to clinics for speech and hearing development exercises.

Today was Friday, so I wasn't going to give up on the exercises so easily—but Conner was staring up at me, his cheeks now fire engine red.

"The airplane goes AAAAAAAHHHHHHHHHHHH!" I said.

Conner's eyes scrunched and he let out a screech. Not only was he maxed out, but I could tell from his body language that he was getting hungry. I rested a hand on my belly as I clumsily got up, picking up Conner and placing him on my hip. I padded into the kitchen as he cried, and quickly strapped him into his high chair. I pulled out a container of last night's dinner—spaghetti and meatballs—from the refrigerator, cut it up, and heated it up just a tiny bit. Finally, I took a seat in front of Conner and swooped a forkful of it in front of him.

"MMMM, YUMMMM YUMMM!" I exclaimed.

He dutifully opened his mouth and gobbled forkful after forkful.

"MMMM, YUMMMMM YUMMMM!"

My belly wobbled as the baby began to kick. I couldn't believe we were already in the home stretch of this pregnancy. Once in a while, in the still of the night, I would let myself feel the pangs of sadness. I knew this was to be expected—life is always busier when you're pregnant with baby two—but I was nostalgic for how I'd gone through pregnancy the first time. I was so fortunate that I tolerated pregnancy exceptionally well, but sometimes it meant that I would almost forget I was pregnant altogether. We were all on autopilot, and for good reason. I never felt much resentment, but I sometimes wished that my bandwidth were greater. I wasn't ready for the pregnancy to be over. I wanted more time with my baby boy resting within my belly, hearing my heartbeat from the inside.

As Conner took his last bite, I glanced at my watch and realized we were running behind. I grabbed a cloth, wiped the sauce off Conner's chin, and quickly scooped him up. Within ten minutes, I had changed Conner's clothes, thrown the diaper bag together, and gotten us into the car. As I navigated onto the highway, my stomach dropped at the congestion ahead. Staring into a sea of illuminated brake lights, I clenched my teeth and gripped the wheel. I wanted to scream.

Nearly an hour later, we'd crawled our way into Seattle in stop-and-go traffic. By the time we walked into OT, I felt like I was ready to die of exhaustion—yet there I was, in a gym surrounded by colorful mats, big foam blocks, and therapists with wide, toothy smiles on their faces. I knew I didn't have time to be tired. I had to be *on*.

"Hi, Conner! Hi, Mom!" Conner's therapist said as she walked toward us with her arms spread wide. She knew Conner loved hugs and cuddles, so she reached for him as he extended his arms. "It's good to see *you*!" she exclaimed, her mannerisms exaggerated. "Follow me, Mom!"

She started leading us to a corner where mats and pillows were all arranged.

"I'm sorry we're a little late," I said.

"Oh, that's okay," she replied. "But I do want to jump right in. Mom, you take a seat right here, and we're going to start with a game of peek-a-boo!" She sat with Conner in her lap, facing me. Knowing the drill, I brought my hands to my face.

"AHHHHHHHHHH, PEEK-A-BOO!" I said.

Conner giggled.

"AAAAAAHHHHHHH, PEEK-A-BOO!" I said again.

"You're doing great, Mom," Conner's therapist added, "but let's try to hold out that 'ahh' a bit longer, okay?"

I took a deep breath, stifling my irritation. I'd been doing exercises with him all day. I didn't understand why she couldn't just step in and do it herself. I was so exhausted, I wanted to give up and go home.

"AHHHHHHHHHHHHHHHHHHHHHHHHH, PEEK-A-BOO!"

"Great job! Mom, you keep working on that with Conner while I get us set up for our next exercise. We're gonna play *forest!*"

She placed Conner on a mat in front of me, then set to work pulling colorful padded columns over in groups and piling more pillows on the floor. I kept playing peek-a-boo with Conner as my anxiety ratcheted up. There were children and parents huddled together all over the place, some children screaming and crying, others laughing hard as they played. There was so much going on—so many sounds and so much stimuli—that I began to feel like I wanted to crawl out of my skin. My palms were clammy and my heart was racing, but I stayed still, covering my face and popping out again and again while Conner smiled. My eyes met his, and I couldn't help but smile too. I drew a breath and stuffed my discomfort deep down inside. In the end, my discomfort didn't matter anyway. I'd do anything for my son.

Nine

T HE WHITE PAPER CRINKLED beneath my thighs while the doctor performed her quick check-up. I stared at the drop ceiling, biting my lower lip.

"I just don't want to be in labor on Christmas," I said. "Or Christmas Eve, you know?"

"I know, Lane, I really do," the doctor replied, standing up from her stool and patting my knee. "I promise we're doing everything we can to move you along."

"I know, and I really appreciate it. You know how it is."

"I do. We just need to be cognizant of the fact that your labor was fast and furious with Conner. You really shouldn't go far, okay?"

I nodded.

"I'll see you soon," she said, stepping out of the room.

"See? She said *soon*," Todd said as I stood up.

"I want soon to be now," I mused, clumsily pulling on my leggings.

It was a Wednesday, and I'd normally be at work, but today I promised to take some time for myself. Todd and I planned to drive to a few of his worksites to check out his new projects one by one before heading to our favorite restaurant for lunch. As we went from site to site, I started to relax. Todd and I operated well together, but it was hard for Todd and me to find time to really connect like we used to. In all the insanity, I didn't often get to see Todd's projects, so it felt special to get to see what he was working so hard on.

At the last site, I was too tired to walk the whole property, so I stayed in the car. Soon, my back began to ache, and I shifted in my seat. Then, I felt it: the familiar swell of pressure. It happened again. And again. Finally, Todd made his way back to the car.

"Todd," I said as he opened the door, "I think I'm in labor."

"Are you sure?" he asked, his eyes wide.

"Pretty sure."

"Okay, call the doctor. We can get to the hospital fast."

I dialed the number and after a brief hold, the doctor came on the line and I explained the situation.

"That was fast!" she said.

"I know," I replied. "What should I do?"

"Come back in and we'll check you. Once we see how dilated you are, we'll go from there. Don't delay though, okay?"

"We won't, we're on our way now!"

Todd sped us back to the doctor's office, threw the car into a parking spot, and opened the door for me. I waddled inside, worried that my water was going to break any moment—all I could think about were those darn paper towels. Soon, I found myself back on the table with the doctor.

"Okay, labor has definitely started, but you're not far along enough to get you admitted to the hospital," she explained. "You can hang tight in our office, and we'll get you into a room where you can wait for things to progress. The hospital birthing rooms are full right now, and this is the best place for you."

Todd helped me gather my things, and we followed the nurse to a nearby room, which was a glorified closet with a bed in it. I lay down and let the contractions wash over me as Todd made all the necessary phone calls to get my mom over to the house to relieve the nanny. Before I knew it, the contractions were coming fast and furious, tearing through me like razor blades. Todd brought the doctor into my closet room. As she checked me, her eyes widened.

"Okay, we have to get you over to the hospital *right now*!"

"Wait, please, I need more time. I want the epidural, I—"

"Lane, we have no time. You're going to be pushing really soon!"

Before I knew it, they were wheeling me out of the closet room into an elevator, rushing me from the doctor's office over to the attached hospital and into Labor and Delivery.

"I'm so sorry, but we still don't have a room available yet," the receptionist said in a low voice after arrived.

"You don't have a room yet!?" I yelled.

"Not yet—just hang tight, we're working on it."

The pain was excruciating; I could barely breathe through it. Todd held my hand as they wheeled me into the hallway where I labored for what felt like hours. Thankfully, the anesthesiologist was able to order the epidural before I got into a room, so I knew it was on the horizon—but that did little to help. Finally, I watched as a woman was wheeled out of a room, her hair matted to her head with sweat, a baby cradled against her chest. A crew ran in after her and began to clean. Pain ripped through me again. And again. And again.

Once the crew finally left, the team wheeled me in with just enough time to get the epidural in place. Barely ten minutes after the epidural kicked in, I was clenching my jaw. I already desperately needed to push.

"I need to push! NOW!"

"Lane, wait!" a nurse called out. "The doctor isn't here yet!"

I gritted my teeth.

The door burst open and the doctor ran in just in time, rubbing sanitizer between her palms, pulling on a pair of gloves, and crouching down between my legs

"Push!" she called out. In the blink of an eye, the baby was out—a boy, who we named Cole. He let out a sharp cry and the doctor placed him on my chest as I panted. He was perfect, pink, and screaming. They wiped him off as Todd cut the cord with tears in the corners of his eyes. I stared down at Cole, letting the love wash over me like ocean waves. Then, it dawned on me.

"The newborn hearing screening!" I cried out. "Please, do the hearing test!"

"We can't do it immediately, but we'll get it ordered just as soon as you're settled in your room," a nurse said. "I promise, we won't delay it."

I drew a breath and tried to calm down. We'd have the test soon. Then we'd know.

I cradled Cole in my arms, my eyes tracing the perfect scoop of his nose and the glint in his tired eyes. Todd placed his arm over my shoulder and leaned into us.

"You did a great job, babe," he said. I nodded.

"I just want to get the test done," I said. "I need to know."

"Soon. It'll be done soon. And you know what? We'll be okay no matter what. We have a healthy baby boy."

"You're right," I said, wincing as the last of the contractions subsided.

The nurses scurried around, getting us cleaned up and ready to move as the doctor finished up. Less than two hours later, we were in our room waiting for the nurse to come get Cole for the hearing test. My throat was tight by the time she arrived. Despite knowing we'd be okay no matter what, I needed to know what our future held. I felt nearly dizzy as the nurse scribbled in Cole's chart. Finally, she smiled.

"This won't take long," she said.

I lay my head back on the bed, then turned to face Todd.

"What will we do if Cole is deaf too?"

"Well," Todd said, fidgeting. "We'd know exactly what to do. We have experience now. We have a team. We have connections. It'll be more of the same, but easier. You know?"

I nodded.

"Good news, Mom and Dad," the nurse said. "His hearing is perfect!" I let out a sob.

Todd rushed to the crib and lifted Cole out, carefully bringing him over to me. Relief mingled with overwhelming, effervescent joy. Todd wrapped his arms around me as I planted a kiss on Cole's head, slowly easing him onto my breast.

Ten

LIFE WITH A BABY and a little boy with special needs took some getting used to, but with our nanny, Todd and I succeeded at managing most everything pretty smoothly, even if I was still exhausted. We treasured every one of Cole's milestones; the experience was so different than what we'd been through with Conner that everything felt new. The first time Cole giggled, we fell into fits of laughter. We cheered when he managed his first roll, celebrated when he was able to sit up on his own, and sighed when he was finally able to support himself on hands and knees. A baby was one thing, but a crawling baby presented a whole new set of challenges.

Late afternoon light streamed through the curtains as I sat in the warm glow of early summer sun. Cole was just six months old; Conner was nearly two years old, sweet and tender as he sidled up to me and peeked down at Cole's face while he snoozed. Conner loved Cole, although he didn't have the words to express it. He reached his hand out and softly touched Cole's head, running his fingers over his downy hair. For an instant, I almost thought Conner would say, "Baby," but instead, he sighed softly and rested his head on my arm.

Conner spent most days at preschool but was always home by the afternoon, when we would sometimes have therapy, sometimes have doctor's appointments, and sometimes have nothing at all. With Conner unable to walk or talk, it was as if I now had two infants with me at all times. I'd do my best to get us all set up in the living room, Cole in his swing or playpen and Conner with pillows and toys, but if I had to put one of them down for a nap, cook a meal, or try to get anything done around the house, I'd have to move the whole operation from one room to the next. Still recovering from the newborn phase and suffering from the exhaustion of around-the-clock feeding, my body felt slow and sluggish. The constant shuffling was draining. I was spent.

In all this, Todd and I each had our roles, and we leaned on our nanny as much as we could. It was now even more difficult for us to connect, as we each had our own set of to-dos and responsibilities. Frankly, I felt numb—like I was just trying to get through each day. After days that were so packed, Todd and I would be together in the evenings, but it felt nearly impossible to focus on one another beyond offering updates in passing. Life was requiring too much for us to really *see* each other. It often felt like we were living life in parallel, our paths barely crossing in any meaningful way.

As the months ticked by, I continued to feel the edges of isolation. Even once I was back at work and our nanny stepped in even further to help juggle things, I still felt like I was slowly disappearing under the weight of it all. Though Todd and I had great friends, it was difficult to feel like we could be completely honest with anyone about how challenging life had become. I didn't want to be the friend who complains constantly, nor did I want anyone to feel bad for us. I still found myself answering questions about how we were doing with short, clipped answers. No matter how we were *really* doing, I always responded, "Fine."

I guess I was fine.

But I wasn't wholly okay.

I stared out the window, watching a butterfly land on a nearby bush. Conner sat up, the magnet dangling off the side of his head. He shook his head as I adjusted it, batting my hands away. His face was scrunched, and he started to wave. I rubbed my eyes, watching him for a few moments longer. It was so hard to discern what he wanted. It often only came through trial and error, which was more difficult now that I had a six-month-old in tow. I worried that a tantrum from Conner would wake Cole, which would throw our whole schedule off.

"Are you tired?" I asked Conner, miming placing my head on a pillow.

He let out a wail.

I did all the usual checks—diaper, water, toys—but his tantrum was coming, roiling beneath the surface. I tried to pull Cole into me to gently shield his ears, but Conner had already thrown himself on the floor and was kicking and screaming. His throat sounded raw as he grabbed at toys and threw them hard across the room. Cole's eyes burst open. He began to cry.

This had to be hunger; there was nothing else to try.

One by one, I moved the boys into the kitchen, getting each of them settled before quickly heading to the cabinet to grab the box of Cheerios. Conner sat in his high chair still crying as I scattered the tiny o's across the tray, and he began shoveling them into his mouth. Cole crawled around in his playpen, hiccupping as he caught his breath. I made Conner's lunch, before sitting down at the table while Conner ate and Cole babbled and grabbed at toys.

I placed pieces of chopped up turkey onto Conner's tray. The house was quiet, but I felt caught in a hellacious storm. I was depleted, unable to get my bearings. I knew deep down that I'd soon come back to earth, but within that calm was a certainty that it would all happen again, and soon.

Once the sun sank below the horizon, I stared at the table, tracing small grooves in the wood where colored pencils had made divots through too-thin sheets of paper. My eyes were heavy and my head throbbed as I reached for a piece of paper and a blunt crayon. I started to jot down a list of challenges we were encountering with Conner in an attempt to get my thoughts straight. I'd found myself in a state where my mind was constantly racing, filled to the brim with questions about what to do next. Clearly, what we were doing was no longer working.

"They're both down," Todd said, walking into the kitchen. He crossed the room, sat in a chair across from me, and raised his eyebrows. "Making a list?"

"I'm trying to. Todd, I think we need to make a change."

"For Conner, you mean?"

"Yes. He had a few major tantrums today, I'm just so—heartbroken for him. I also spoke with the school yesterday. He had another huge tantrum in the classroom. That's four this week so far. He's still unable to communicate, and he's not standing or walking. I mean, he's two-and-a half. We're getting to the point where we need to do our individualized education plan anyway. Could we—"

"Maybe try a different school?" he suggested.

"I think we need to consider it. The drive is so, so long, and he's still struggling like crazy."

"Okay," he said. "Are you sure? Is there anything else we can try?"

"I can't see how we can keep doing this. What's the point?"

"You're right. We can look into the Seattle School District. I remember reading that they have a program to teach how to sign exact English. Maybe that'll get him over the hump without confusing things too much. We can keep up with the auditory-verbal therapy with Listen & Talk at the same time."

"I think this is the right move," I said, reaching for Todd's hand. He nodded.

"We'll get things going tomorrow."

Within a few days, we were able to get in for a tour of the Seattle School District preschool. Much like Listen & Talk, the rooms were bright and colorful, filled with arts and crafts and big, bright charts and packed with books, puzzles, and an array of educational toys. The staff was kind and knowledgeable, and the entire place felt like home. Now six months old, Cole was able to go to daycare and spend his days in the infant room with kind care providers who loved him so well.

Since the school was only twenty minutes away from the house and the fact that they provided a bus service, the convenience was transformative. The boys were no longer spending hours in the car each day, which made an immediate and huge difference for Conner, whose tantrums had slowed considerably. He was now three years old and calmer, becoming frustrated less frequently and better able to focus. Although he still wasn't walking, it was becoming easier for me to supervise both boys at once. Conner was maturing.

One afternoon after school, I poured myself a cup of water and headed into the living room. I was exhausted from a full day of work—running between meetings before darting to school to pick the boys up early to head to an appointment downtown. Cole was now on the floor of the living room clapping along to an episode of *Blue's Clues*. Conner was crawling over a big mound of pillows, laughing as he let himself fall headfirst into the massive mound of fluff. He wiggled and kicked as I picked him up and took him across the room, sat him in front of me, and pulled the basket of toys over. I reached in and grabbed the airplane—my usual starting point. "The airplane goes AHHHHHHHHHHH!" I began.

Conner looked at me and cocked his head.

"The airplane goes AHHHHHHHHHHHH!" I repeated.

"AHHHHHHHHHHHHHH!" he parroted.

My breath caught.

"Conner! Oh my gosh, Conner! Try it again! The airplane goes AHHHHHHHHHH!"

"AHHHHHHHHHHHHHHH!" My chest felt ready to burst. I picked up the cow and held it in front of him.

"The cow goes MOOOOOOOOOOO!" I said.

"OOOOOOOOOOO!" he parroted.

"You're doing it, you're doing it!" I cried out.

He smiled wide, kicking his feet excitedly.

"MAMA!" I said, pointing at myself, "MAMA!"

"MMMM!" he parroted.

I reached forward and scooped him into my arms. I couldn't believe it! Something had clicked, right then and there. I reached for another toy.

"The car goes RRRR, BEEP BEEP!"

"ROOOOOOOOOOO!" he said back.

Cole crawled over to see what the excitement was about, climbing over Conner to make his way into my lap. I reached for the phone and dialed Todd as quickly as I could. As soon as he answered I shouted, "Todd! Listen! The airplane goes AHHHHHHHHHHHH!"

"AHHHHHHH!" Conner replied.

"Buddy! You're *doing it*!" Todd yelled on the other end. "I'm coming home right now!"

I put the phone down and moved Cole back onto the carpet, where he gathered a plastic shark and a pickup truck in his hands as I squeezed Conner.

"You're getting it," I whispered. "I can't believe it. I just can't believe it."

Eleven

I SAT ON THE floor next to Conner's bed, my hand making small circles on his back. I glanced over at Cole, who was fast asleep, sprawled out with one leg dangling off the side of his twin-sized bed. Conner's breath became slow and steady, and soon, he let out a soft sigh. I carefully removed my hand from his back, pushed myself up, and crept into the hallway. Before I could open the door to my bedroom, Conner let out a sharp scream. I spun and bolted back into the boys' room, making my way in the dark to Conner's side and stooping down next to him.

"What's wrong, buddy?" I asked.

Conner's cheeks were wet with tears; the neck of his Spiderman pajamas was already damp. He waved his hands and shook his head violently as he grabbed at my shirt and wrapped his arms around me. I went through the mental list of things that could be bothering him but came up blank. That's when my eyes fell on the closed bathroom door. I shook my head as it dawned on me: I'd forgotten to flip the light on and crack the door before leaving the room. Conner was completely panicked, sobbing so hard that his face felt hot against my shoulder.

"It's okay, nothing is going to hurt you," I promised, knowing he couldn't hear me because he didn't sleep with his earpiece on. "Let's get up and turn the light on now."

Conner was so heavy that I struggled to get myself up with him wrapped around my midsection, but I managed to get to my feet and cross the room. He buried his head in my shoulder as my hand searched the wall for the switch and flicked it on.

"See, there's the light. Nothing to be afraid of."

He opened his eyes wide and scanned the room. His breathing slowed. I moved to the bed and eased him back onto the mattress where he quickly snuggled beneath his comforter and sighed. I sat next to him and rubbed his back until I felt his heart rate slow. I didn't even try to stand until he let out a small snore. Finally, I padded down the hallway into my room, where Todd was waiting for me. He paused the TV as I sank onto my side of the bed.

"Everything okay?" he asked.

"Yeah," I responded. "I forgot to leave the bathroom light on."

"How *could* you?" he replied with a smirk.

"I know," I said, rubbing my eyes.

I leaned back against the headboard and let my body relax. The exhaustion was so overwhelming at times that it felt like I was living on pure momentum. I had become adept at keeping my head down and powering through, letting the cadence of the day sweep me up and carry me from task to task, appointment to appointment. But in the dead of the night when all was quiet, I felt the dull ache behind my eyes.

Despite the seemingly never-ending busyness that gripped our lives, we were beginning to see some real breaks in the clouds. Conner's speech was progressing, and he was making big strides in OT. Best of all, his clumsy walking seemed to be much better now, which was a welcome change. Cole was progressing on his milestones quickly, which meant he was surpassing Conner in many ways, but his love for Conner was so strong that he always remained by his side. I'd smile watching them toddle around the kitchen together. My heart was so full seeing Conner's steady progress; I finally felt like I could let go of some of the nagging fears that seemed to control my life. But life is funny; sometimes, you let go of one fear only to find another lying in wait.

The sky was bright blue and cloudless as we walked through the park's sprawling, white gates. Todd placed Cole on the ground as Conner kicked and wiggled, struggling to get out of his stroller. The boys bumped elbows; Cole grabbed Conner's hand and they raced ahead together. Todd and I picked up our pace, smiling at one another. I felt tears in my eyes as we rounded a corner and the castle came into view. Conner was all arms and legs, scrambling as quickly as he could to keep up with Cole. Together, they stopped short, standing shoulder to shoulder as they stared up at the spires.

"So cool, right?" Todd asked.

"Wow!" Cole responded. "Let's go see *Mickey!*"

We put the boys in their double stroller, which Todd and I took turns pushing as we made our way further into the park, past swirling rides and stands selling hot dogs, fried dough, and ice cream cones that required two hands. Puffing, we headed toward the attractions for little kids. There was the flying Dumbo ride, swirling teacups, bumper cars, small rollercoasters, and a log flume with water cascading from the sides.

"Slow down, Cole!" Todd called as Cole raced toward a stand selling Mickey ears.

Soon Todd and I were panting as we hopped from ride to ride with the boys. Their joy was palpable, and my heart filled with so much happiness that I had to hold back tears. We let the boys lead, jogging behind them as they ran, hopped up on more sugar than I cared to admit. Soon, they were red-faced and began to tire, leaning against us as we walked in desperate need of a break.

"I have an idea," I said to Todd. "Let's hit the 'It's a Small World' ride. It'll be nice and cool in there."

"Great idea. Boys, let's get on a boat!"

We pushed our way through the turnstiles with a *clank* and took our place in line, each of us toting one of the boys, their heads on each of our shoulders. We crept toward the entrance, flinching as we grazed shoulders with other sweaty park-goers. When we finally reached the door, a swathe of cool air draped over my shoulders. As the line before us shrunk into the building, Conner's body stiffened. It took my eyes a moment to adjust to the dim lighting. The further we walked, the darker it became. Soon, Conner's head snapped up, and his grip around me tightened like a vice. Cole cocked his head. Conner began to scream, his wails so sharp they cut the air like shards of glass.

"It's okay, it's just pretend," Todd said, placing his hand on Conner's back.

Conner began to kick and swing his arms, beating them against me as I tried to steady myself.

"Conner, it's all right," I said. "It's just another ride!"

He was kicking so hard that I nearly lost my breath. I quickly hoisted him further onto my shoulder and pushed my way back through the line, racing out as fast as I could. Daylight burst in as I pushed my way through the emergency exit, causing the alarm's shrill screams to pierce the air. Conner stopped kicking as soon as we got outside. I made my way to a bench with him, his body collapsing against mine as he tried to steady himself. I cradled his head and stared into his red-rimmed eyes.

"What was that about, buddy?"

"Mama," he responded. "Mama."

I held him close to my chest, a lump forming in my throat as I let the truth overwhelm me. Though things had been starting to feel easier, our problems were becoming everlasting. They followed us everywhere we went—even the happiest place on earth.

After several days at Disney, we returned home exhausted, sunburned, and ready to get back into our regular routine. I'd spent the rest of the trip with my eyes trained on Conner, finally letting myself really think about the depths of his fear of the dark. It had always been an issue, but it had suddenly reached a fever pitch. After attempting the "It's A Small World" ride, we were unable to do any dim indoor rides as a family; either or I would stay outside with Conner while the other took Cole and zoomed off. In our hotel room, we had to sleep with so many lights on that it was like sleeping outside at noon. I couldn't help but think back to when Conner was a baby—the way we vacuumed around him, the way we thought he was just so easy-going. The way we were so *oblivious* to his struggles.

The day after we arrived home, I called the pediatrician's office and explained what was going on to the nurse, who was quick to dismiss my fears.

"I know, Mom, it can be really stressful when these fears pop up in our kids."

I gritted my teeth. I hated when they called me *Mom*.

"I'm sure it's absolutely nothing, but the doctor has let me know that she will send over a referral," she continued. "There's an eye doctor nearby that many of our patients use. You can make an appointment and get some tests done to ease your mind."

It was barely two days before I found myself sitting in a chair in the optometrist's office with Conner on my lap. Dr. O'Brien was a younger man with dark hair and kind eyes. He eased his rolling stool in front of us and leaned forward.

"Conner, I'm going to place some drops in your eyes, okay?" he asked.

Conner tried to hide his head beneath my arms.

"It's okay, buddy," I assured him, "this will be quick."

Conner kicked and squirmed, letting out huge screams and roars. Finally, Dr. O'Brien maneuvered himself directly beside me. I felt sick as I held Conner's head in place and Dr. O'Brien managed to get his eyes open and squeeze a drop into each one. Conner kicked and screeched, furiously rubbing his eyes. Moments later, Dr. O'Brien asked him to open his eyes wide and shone a bright light into each one. His forehead crinkled as he stared into the lens of the retinoscope.

"So, you say he's been displaying fear in dark spaces?"

"Not just fear, it's more than that—he becomes absolutely hysterical."

"I see," Dr. O'Brien replied. The stool rattled as he rolled backwards. He dug into his drawer and pulled out several cards. "And he's had issues with hearing since birth, correct?"

"Yes, we received the profound deafness diagnosis when he was a little over six months old."

"Got it. All right. Does he know his animals yet?"

"Yes, he knows the sounds they make."

He signaled that I should have Conner look through the lenses.

"Conner, what animals do you see on the third line down?" he asked.

Conner looked around the room, then down at his feet.

"Buddy," I prodded, "Look: row one, two, three. What animals are on that row? You know these."

He said nothing.

"Okay, what about the line above it?" the doctor asked.

Conner tilted his head and said, "WOOF, WOOF!"

The doctor asked about the pictures line by line, each one stumping Conner, who I could tell was reaching his limit. I tightened my grip around him as he wiggled, trying to kick free. Dr. O'Brien rolled away from the counter.

"I'm going to run out and look up a couple of different things," he said. "You two hang tight, and I'll be right back."

Conner made his way to the floor and began fiddling with wires and pressing buttons on the side of the chair. I chewed the inside of my cheeks. Aside from his fear of the dark, we hadn't noticed anything out of the ordinary. I reasoned that must've meant his vision couldn't be too bad; if it were, we would have seen the signs. I imagined the doctor coming in with a light prescription and began to think about what color glasses would look best on his little face. Blue? Red? Black? Would he keep them on, or would it be a battle? How would we juggle the glasses and his implant? Would they both fit over his ears?

Conner pressed a bright red button, causing the chair to tilt back as the door opened and the doctor breezed back into the room. I scooped Conner up off the floor and brought him back into my lap. As he wriggled, I awkwardly pressed the button again to make the chair whir back into place. Dr. O'Brien doctor sat on the stool holding a small stack of papers. He leaned forward and cleared his throat.

"Mrs. McKittrick," he said, "I'm sorry to be so abrupt—but have you heard of Usher syndrome?" I bounced Conner on my knee as he reached for a cord on the chair, grabbing my hair as I guided his hand away.

"I'm sorry, have I heard of what?"

"Usher syndrome—it's an extremely rare genetic disorder."

I swallowed hard.

"I don't want to cause undue fear," the doctor continued, "but I did notice some concerning signs when I examined his retina. It could be nothing, but considering the fact that he's also got issues with his hearing, we have to consider the possibility."

My mind flashed to a VHS tape Conner's audiologist had given us following the deaf diagnosis. I suddenly remembered a portion of the video that focused on a deafblind adult—he had from Usher syndrome. As the scene unfolded, I felt, at the time, *relieved*. Despite having to process the harrowing news that Conner was deaf, I was grateful that we weren't dealing with blindness, too.

But now, here we were.

My chest tightened, and I felt light of breath.

"I don't know what to do," I managed. "What do I do?"

"First, I'm going to prescribe Conner a pair of eyeglasses. Then, I'm going to get you in with a colleague who has dealt with Usher syndrome in other patients of hers. I know this is scary, but we don't know anything for certain. One step at a time."

The doctor handed me a stack of papers as I hoisted Conner onto my hip. The world became a swirl of colors, a splatter painting of ice blue panic. I managed to get out of the office and strap Conner into the car. On my way back to work, I know I dropped Conner somewhere—with the nanny or at school—but my memory couldn't hold onto the details. I was completely unmoored. Before I knew it, I was sitting in my office at my desk, which was littered with papers. I stared at the post-its, blending with nearby paper scraps and piles of contracts that needed to be signed. My mind couldn't focus; I wasn't there. Instead of being connected to the real world, I was lost in the undertow of a tidal wave.

It could have been a moment or several hours later that I vaguely registered a knock at my office door. I looked up to see my colleague, Ashley, standing in the doorway, looking at me quizzically.

"Lane, I just stopped by to give you that file you asked for," she said. She hesitated before taking a few steps forward. "How did the appointment with the eye doctor go?"

I didn't know Ashley well; she was someone I just considered a work colleague, but the question caused my roiling emotions to burst out of me like lava from a violent volcano. I sobbed loudly, my head in my hands and my shoulders shaking.

"Awful," I said. "It's all awful. Conner—they think he has something awful. Usher syndrome. He's deaf, and it's making him go blind too." All the air was leaving me, and I couldn't stop the sobs from overwhelming my body. Ashley crossed the room and stooped down by my side, setting the file on my desk and her hand on my back.

"Oh, Lane," she said. "I can't imagine."

I wanted to shake her hand from my back, to push her away, curl into a cocoon, and cry myself into oblivion. She stood stock-still, whispering words of encouragement that filled me with rage. My breath caught as I waved her away.

"I need a minute, please," I said finally.

"Okay, let me get you some water," she said, scurrying out of the room.

I suddenly realized that I'd been in such shock that I hadn't called Todd yet. I grabbed my Blackberry and managed to dial his number through the tears.

"Hey, babe," he answered. "How was the appointment?"

For what seemed like several minutes, I couldn't get any words out. I still felt like I couldn't breathe as I held back sobs.

"It was really bad, babe," I said. "The doctor thinks—he thinks he will also go blind. Conner may have Usher syndrome." There was a moment of silence as Todd absorbed my words and their significance.

"Lane, what do you mean? What is Usher syndrome? There's no way, he can't—"

"He can. The doctor looked at his retina and..."

Crinkles and soft static came from the other end of the line as Todd began to cry. I became hysterical, feeling as if my entire life was spiraling out of control. There was nothing I could do. I was so overcome that I didn't know what to say, so I told him I'd see him at home soon and put the phone down. Ashley came back in the room with a bottle of water and a cookie from the break room.

"Thanks," I murmured, putting the cookie in the trash can the moment she shut the door behind her. Nothing around me seemed real; I trembled with the vulnerability of a character in a horror movie who knows there's an ax-wielding maniac lying in wait.

Eventually, my boss came by and encouraged me to leave for the day, but it took me until the sun was low in the sky to pick up my bag and drag myself out into the parking lot—that long to feel like I could move, let alone drive. In a fog, I merged onto the highway before my eyes drifted to the passenger's seat where I'd tossed the papers the doctor had handed me. On top was the prescription for glasses. Conner *needed* them—while he still had his vision, it needed to be as crisp as possible. I had to get them, and fast. Realizing I was nearing home, I threw the wheel to the right and peeled off into the nearest exit lane, my tires rumbling as I drifted back onto the side streets.

Before I knew it, Todd, Conner, and I were standing in LensCrafters staring at endless rows of glasses in all shapes and sizes. Comparatively, the kids' section was small—just a couple of rows with low mirrors positioned nearby. Conner's eyes landed on a blue pair of designer glasses. They were more expensive than I wanted them to be, but I didn't care. With all that he was going through, Conner deserved the best of the best.

I grabbed the frames and rushed to the counter. A young, red-haired associate stood at the register, smiling at me as she took the frames from my hands.

"If this is all, I just need to see the prescription so we can get things rolling," she said.

I slid the now-crinkled paper across the counter.

"All right, it looks like we can have these ready for you tomorrow around noon."

"Tomorrow?" I echoed. "No, I need them *now*."

"Ma'am, I'm sorry. We're just an hour away from closing, so we can't—"

"Please, I need you to do this today. My son, he's having trouble. I just found out that my son is going to go blind. I need to get these to him as soon as I can. Just please, please see what you can do."

"But we're closing, and—"

"I don't care," I snapped. She blinked at me in shock, and I took a gasping breath. Todd lay his hand on my shoulder. "Please," I said, softer. "I'm begging you."

"Okay," the associate acquiesced. "Let me just talk to our tech team."

We took our seats in the chairs lining the wall near the exam room. As I stared across the store, I caught sight of myself in a nearby mirror. My eyes were bloodshot with big, dark circles beneath them. My skin was pale, my cheeks chapped and stained red. Even my hair was frizzy and disheveled. I looked like I'd come unglued, and I had.

The sales associate nodded at me as the technicians in the lab rushed to make Conner's lenses. My heart rate slowed and my breathing returned to normal. At the very least, I'd accomplished one thing that day that would make life slightly easier for Conner. My mind tightened around that thought. Life would be anything but easy for my little boy. There was nothing I could do about it but pick up the pieces and try to glue them back together, one by one.

Twelve

THAT EVENING, TODD AND I found ourselves at our usual spots at the kitchen table. We'd both had such intense breakdowns during the day that we dutifully let the silence drape over us. My eyes ached, my ears were ringing, and my body felt heavy under the weight of the new list of *what ifs* in my mind. I'd become well-versed in living with deafness; we'd made such good headway, built an amazing team, and had a busy, but enriching schedule for Conner. Now, that entire routine would likely need to be overhauled, compounded with the fact that I knew next to nothing about blindness. All I could think about was the white cane, dark glasses, and guide dogs. My only points of reference were stories of Hellen Keller and that damn VHS tape.

"Okay, so we get the appointment with the retinal specialists, and we go from there," Todd said finally, his brow furrowed.

"What's the point?" I asked. "We know it's true."

"I know, I really do. But it's our best next step."

"I just feel so helpless. We'll have to start from scratch, we need a new IEP..." I said, overwhelmed at the thought of it all. "How are we going to do this?" He grabbed my hands.

"We're going to do what we always do. We're going to get through this and do what's best for Conner. We figured it out before, we can figure it out again."

"Do we need to find a new school? Do we need to find new doctors, new—?"

"One step at a time. We'll see the specialist to confirm what we know, but in the meantime, we'll start having conversations. We can do this."

I nodded, pulling away from Todd's grip to rub my eyes with the palms of my hands. I pushed the chair away from the table and shuffled into the bedroom, where I buried myself beneath the covers and cried myself to sleep, shutting the world out—even Todd.

Within two weeks, word had spread about Conner's diagnosis. It was hard to receive phone calls and texts filled with sympathy and concern; as always, I wanted to appear strong and tough. I had everything under control and didn't want anyone to take pity on Conner or our family. I did my best to give our loved ones honest updates without letting my emotions leak into conversations. I was measured when I spoke; I didn't speculate or engage when I heard the tone shifting to sorrow. I simply got through each conversation one by one.

The most difficult conversations to navigate were those with parents and friends within the deaf and hard of hearing community. Whenever I heard the phrase, "I heard about Conner—I'm just so sorry," my throat would tighten. I would nod and whisper *Thank you*, but inside, I felt like I was dying. Amid all those saccharine smiles and soft nods, I knew what they were thinking: *Thank God it's not my kid*. I couldn't take their wide eyes staring at me and their hands placed on my knees or shoulders, offering support that felt all wrong. No one really understood. No one had advice that could get us anywhere. Once again, we were in uncharted territory with nowhere to turn. Yet, we still had to go through the motions. The official diagnosis was yet to come.

Although staring at Conner in a hospital gown was becoming routine, it never got any easier. Conner was mobile now and so much more aware of things going on around him. He was no longer a tiny baby beneath stiff, white sheets. He was a little boy, scared of needles and doctors in white coats, just like his mom. The process of having him sedated this time was much the same, but since he was bigger now, the tantrums were more difficult to manage. I found myself sweating, tugging at the sleeves of my itchy wool sweater as the doctor managed to ease the mask over his mouth and nose.

It was early November, and we'd somehow been finding our way through swirls of anxiety peppered with pumpkin carving and candy. Todd and I had discovered Foundation Fighting Blindness, which was the only resource on Usher syndrome that we could find. The website had very little information, but it did share a list of retinal-specialized ophthalmologists, which included a well-respected doctor in Portland. It would be more than a three-hour drive for his electroretinogram (ERG), but we didn't care; we knew we needed someone who didn't just understand blindness, but Usher syndrome, too. The test wasn't dissimilar to the ABR test Conner underwent to determine deafness. Conner would be sedated as the team placed thin fiber electrodes in contact with the cornea, probes that would record retinal activity.

Various tests would be performed during the procedure with light. The retina's reaction, or lack thereof, would lead to an accurate vision diagnosis.

Todd, Conner, and I were ushered into a pitch-black room, where we were told to wait for about an hour for Conner's eyes to prepare for the ERG—until Conner fell asleep. The blackness of the room was making me claustrophobic, and I had hit my limit. I needed to let Todd handle this. The staff ushered me out of the room, into the hallway, and back into the waiting room. My head throbbed as I perched on the faux leather chairs, surrounded by large, artful prints of eyes, which felt poetic in the worst way. I picked at my nails, trying to tap out emails on my Blackberry and flipping through a book I'd brought, but feeling unable to focus. Despite my anxiety, I knew in my heart that this test was pointless. Todd and I had already settled into the diagnosis, and the news had spread. We were already making headway on building a new team. This test was us doing our due diligence.

Soon, the nurse called, and I raced back into Conner's room amid a flurry of activity. There he was, sitting on Todd's lap, his soft brown hair shining in the halogen light. Dr. Wells came in just as I was gathering Conner in my arms.

"Mr. and Mrs. McKittrick, I know this is a scary moment for you, but Conner did really well throughout the procedure," he said.

Before Dr. Wells had a chance to speak, Todd blurted, "It's Usher, right?"

"As you know, the test uses several metrics to determine the status of a patient's vision. In examining his responses throughout the testing, I am certain that this is Usher syndrome we're seeing. The eye disorder is called Retinitis Pigmentosa, which we call RP. Usher syndrome is a combination of hearing loss and RP, and your son's RP is progressive. Because of how it's presenting, we believe Conner has Usher syndrome type 1, but that can only be confirmed by genetic testing."

"Okay, so how bad is his vision now?" I asked.

"Although Conner does show some loss in his rods, which are the photoreceptors that provide vision during dim or night, it seems that the progression is fairly slow. Per the results of the previous test done by your eye doctor in Washington, Conner's central vision can be corrected with glasses at the moment. Of course, we'll need to monitor his rod and cone cell loss closely over time. This disease is progressive, as you know, so we need to stay on top of it."

I nodded.

"I knew it was Usher—we both did—but it's surreal to hear you say all this," Todd said, rubbing his eyes.

"I know this is a lot to process. The thing is though, so much research is being done on Usher syndrome at the moment that there really is hope for a cure, maybe sooner rather than later. We just need to stay the course, monitor, and take this all as it comes."

Dr. Wells pulled up a chair and sat down with us, answering every question we had. He never once glanced at his watch or fidgeted, nor did he look longingly at the door. He was focused and kind, compassionate and committed to sharing every bit of information he had. We told him about redoing Conner's Individualized Education Program (IEP) and all the ways we hoped to build a community. He nodded and leaned forward.

"You know," he began, "I work closely with a group of researchers associated with Boys Town University who may be able to do the genetics testing. That's your next step—genetic screening. Let me reach out and see what I can find out for you."

"Yes, please," I replied.

"They will probably have us draw blood. Then, they will run tests, and we'll assign you a genetics counselor to go over the results. You'll be in great hands, but I'm here too. I'll see you periodically to redo these tests, and I'm happy to help any way I can."

Conner began to stir, repeating, "Mama, Mama." Todd rushed to the side of the bed and kissed the top of his head. I pulled Conner into me, resting his head against my chest. As hard as it was to hear the official diagnosis, it came with a sense of relief. We had our answers. We could see a path forward. Now, all we had to do was put one foot in front of the other.

A few weeks later, we sat at a small desk across from a young female genetics counselor with neatly combed black hair and milky white skin.

"First of all, I have to say that you're both doing so well," she said. "I know this diagnosis isn't easy to swallow, but you're doing everything right as far as I can see."

"To be honest, as soon as the eye doctor brought it up the first time, we knew it was Usher," Todd said. "We've dealt with so many challenges for so long, we just—"

His voice broke.

"I know it's a tough diagnosis to process, and answers are extremely hard to come by," the counselor continued. "Our understanding of the disease is in its infancy, but the team here has dedicated countless hours to increase our understanding. Let me dig into our findings. I'll explain Usher syndrome to you as it pertains to genetics, but please stop me if you have any questions."

Todd and I remained perched on the edge of our seats as she placed sheets of paper on her desk, each displaying a different chart that broke down the genetics of the disease. She explained that Usher syndrome was a rare disease that had a two-pronged effect—it caused deafness and an eye disease called retinitis pigmentosa or RP, which caused blindness. It impacted individuals differently and led to a myriad of symptoms and challenges, one of the most common of which were struggles with balance.

She explained that Usher syndrome commonly ran in families, passed down by the parents. It was caused by mutations in certain genes that related to sight, hearing, and balance. Depending on the mutation, symptoms varied, but everyone who lives with Usher would struggle with some combination of certain issues. Finally, she explained that there were nine genes that caused the three different types of Usher syndrome.

The Type 1 genes were MY07A, USH1C, CDH23, PCHD15, and USH1G.

Type 2 genes were USH2A, GPR98, and WHRN.

And the Type 3 gene was CLRN1.

Usher syndrome could only be passed down to a child if both parents had an extremely rare mutation called autosomal recessive inheritance. Finally, she explained that Conner had Usher syndrome type 1B.

"So, what do we do?" I asked, my head heavy with the volume of information.

"I'm going to give you a list of resources, and I'd like to connect you with someone local who has Usher," she said. "He's worked within the hospital system for years. I think connecting with him may ease your mind—I'm sure there are so many questions he can answer for you."

"We'll email him," Todd said with a nod.

"Listen, I also want you to know that we are actively looking for a cure. Funds are limited, so it's been challenging to make headway, but we're working on it. There is hope."

My stomach flipped.

Twenty minutes later, we opened the clinic's sliding glass door with a *whoosh*, and the frigid air wrapped itself around us. I gazed at the sky as we made our way to the car. True to form for Washington winters, it had been overcast for days, the sky dishwater gray and heavy with rain. But as I squinted at the clouds overhead, the sun began to break from behind the gunmetal. I paused to let the rays warm my skin before opening the passenger door of our car.

Here we were, having received confirmation that we were dealing with an insidious, unforgiving disease—yet, I suddenly felt better than I had in years. The burden of having a lack of information had finally been lifted. We knew exactly what we were dealing with and why. Now, it was time to fight.

As our life reshaped itself around our new truth, one word kept us moving forward, spurring us on: *cure*. We'd now heard it from two different specialists who were busy searching for answers. There was hope, but things needed to move faster for Conner's sake. He was missing out on so much due to the limitations of his disease, and Todd and I couldn't sit idly by and wait.

As time went on, we were consistently asked by friends and family what they could do to help. Most wanted to donate to the cause, but we had nowhere to send them. It soon became clear that a foundation would give us somewhere to funnel that support, with the added benefit of allowing us to build community. Instead of staying up at night worrying, crying, and consoling one another, Todd and I became a united force. We would build a foundation that filled a massive existing gap. We would be the ones to gather information, compile resources, and raise enough money to push research ahead as quickly and efficiently as possible.

One sunny afternoon right after the diagnosis, Todd and I were at our beach cabin with my mom. She nodded along as Todd and I told her about all our hopes for our foundation, how we'd run it and all the good we could do.

"I know it sounds crazy, but we really could make a huge difference," I said. "We have no idea what we're doing with this diagnosis. The Usher community needs connection. We need collaboration, and researchers need funds to make headway."

"It's a fantastic idea," she replied.

"It feels like the right path," Todd added, "and everyone wants to help. This provides people with an inroad to actually *do* something."

"So, what about the name 'Hear See Hope'?" my mom asked.

"I love it," I said, placing one hand over my heart. "It's so hopeful and bright—not heavy. It's perfect."

With hope stirring within me, I watched as trees dotted with sprouting buds streaked past the window. I placed my hand on Cole's knee; he fiddled with his favorite stuffed bear, patches of its fur loved right off. Conner's eyes drifted to the window. He pushed his glasses up and scrunched his eyes. I wondered what the world looked like to my little boy. I imagined green leaves and blue skies going dark around the edges, but I quickly refocused on the foundation and all the good we could do. Todd and I would be Conner's superheroes. And we wouldn't stop until a cure was found.

Thirteen

I SAT ON THE couch as Conner and Cole tussled on the floor in a patch of dappled sunlight that streamed in through the window. My workday had been brutal. After nearly a dozen meetings and putting out several fires, I was fully depleted. To top it all off, I'd received a call from school that Conner had had another huge tantrum—this one more earth-shattering than the last.

My tired mind drifted to the recent lunch we'd had with Will, the man with Usher syndrome our genetic counselor had connected us with. Three days earlier, Todd and I had driven into the city to meet him at a small café near the hospital. Will was a man in his 50s, wearing dark sunglasses and sitting with a white cane propped up against a nearby wall. As we made our way to his table, I softly touched his back.

"Thank you for meeting with us," I said. "I'm Lane, and this is Todd."

We pulled out chairs and sat, then quickly ordered coffees. We exchanged small talk about where we lived, how Conner was doing, and where we were in the process. I couldn't help but clench my jaw and stare at my reflection in Will's glasses as he spoke. It was the first time I had met anyone who had used a white cane. It scared me.

"I want you to know: I'm happy," he said. "I have a job I love and a wonderful family. This diagnosis isn't the end of the world by any means."

I stared back at him, trying to force myself to say something—to ask a question, share more about our experience, *anything*—yet somehow, my mind couldn't make the connection between this man and my son. All I could think about was the fact that Conner would never have to live life the way Will had been forced to. We were so much closer to a cure than Will had ever been when he was growing up. There was hope for Conner where Will had had none. We told Will about the foundation and welcomed him to participate in any way he felt comfortable. There was progress to be made, and we'd spearhead it all.

I sat lost in thought as the boys continued to wrestle. Cole let out a small cry as Conner snatched a toy from him, but he didn't wallow in frustration. Instead, he reached for a toy car and drove it over his outstretched legs; his knees were mountains, his shins the valleys. When he was done, he carefully handed the car to Conner and showed him how to maneuver it over his legs, too. I loved watching them together, seeing how beautifully connected they were. Cole was the little brother, but he was the caretaker in many ways. It was the role Cole was born to play, and he did so beautifully, with more love in his heart than I could have ever hoped.

Between rushing the boys to and from school, tackling our usual appointments, re-tooling our Individualized Education Plan (IEP) with our counselor, and getting the foundation up and running, Todd and I became like two ships passing in the night. Although we worked closely together on the foundation, we each filled our own roles and accomplished our tasks independently. We navigated the process of getting Hear See Hope set up as a non-profit, handled all of the paperwork, and were officially ready for our first fundraiser by the time spring was in full swing. After much back and forth, we finally finished the website, which was centered around the mission statement we had painstakingly crafted:

"Our mission is to help find a cure for Usher syndrome, the most common cause of deafblindness in the U.S. 99% of the money we raise goes toward research. We are a 501(c)3 not-for-profit organization in search of funds to sustain the fight against Usher syndrome."

As news continued to spread about Conner's diagnosis, we were still receiving a steady stream of calls, texts, and emails from people offering to help. Sometimes I had to work to swallow that prickly feeling that welled inside me anytime I heard that phrase: "I'm so sorry for what you're going through."

In the meantime, Todd and I were working closely with our team of doctors. Dr. Wells was an invaluable resource and quickly became a core part of our team, which we continued to grow carefully and intentionally. Each and every member of the team—including the genetics counselor—was ready and willing to help in any way they could.

As things began to take shape, Todd spearheaded our very first event for Hear See Hope. Reflecting on our experience and taking into account all the questions we fielded from friends and family, we came up with an idea that we hoped would become an invaluable resource for others. With help from Todd's brother, who was a filmmaker, we set out to make a short film explaining Usher syndrome, giving insight into the work being done and the hope for a cure on the horizon.

Over two weeks, Todd meticulously organized an interview schedule, coordinating camera crews, doctors, and geneticists, and of course, us. Everyone filmed their interviews one at a time except for Todd and me, who sat in front of the camera in side-by-side chairs. My palms began to sweat as I stared into the lens, stammering as I answered questions. Through tears, I managed to share our experience, explain the needs we had, and express hope that there was a solution out there that we only needed to find. As the camera went down and I brushed tears from my face, it felt as though a weight had been lifted off my shoulders. I'd been asked countless questions by countless people over the years and had been so reserved and careful to appear strong that it felt good to be able to speak openly and honestly. As we wrapped filming, I found solace in the fact that we were moving in the exact right direction. We were informing others, searching for answers, and empowering others to fund the research we so desperately needed to move forward.

When the night of the event finally arrived, we walked into the still and quiet theater to set up. We placed a folding table up front with information about the foundation, setting up another for drinks and refreshments. Together, we stood at the front of the theater as friends and family streamed in. We greeted guests one at a time, giving them warm hugs and expressing our thanks. My stomach turned as Will walked into the room and made his way over to us. He reached out his hand, shaking mine and then Todd's.

"Conner is so lucky to have you," he said with a smile. "I wish Hear See Hope had been around when I was younger. My parents needed something like this so badly."

"We appreciate you coming tonight," Todd said. "Let me help you to your seat."

Todd placed his hand on Will's back and guided him away. I watched as partygoers locked eyes on him as he moved through the theater. I swallowed hard as they began to make the connection. I had to stifle a rising urge to explain to everyone that Conner would never be in that situation. It would never get that far; there was *hope*. I steadied myself as Todd joined me at the front of the room. He checked his watch.

"Everyone, if you can please take your seats, we're excited to begin," he called out. The crowd grew quiet as everyone made their way to their seats. "We are so grateful to everyone who's here this evening. When we started on this journey, we had no idea what to expect. A lot of that stemmed from the fact that so little information on Usher syndrome exists, and what does exist is incredibly hard to understand. Many people diagnosed with the syndrome are left with a list of questions and nowhere to turn—yet there is so much hope. In working closely with a team of experts, Lane and I are committed to empower medical professionals to make headway toward a cure."

The crowd applauded.

"A cure is on the horizon," Todd continued. "We hope you enjoy the film we worked so hard to put together. It'll answer all the questions you have and give you an idea of what the funds we raise will go toward. We love and appreciate you all so much."

The crowd applauded once more as the lights dimmed. As images flickered across the screen, a sense of excitement washed over me, mingled with a sense of pride. I thought back to the old VHS tape, the grainy image of the man staring into the camera and explaining his struggles. Now, seeing our film in vivid color, I realized we were providing something vital to a community that had been so widely ignored. We would inform others. We would race for a cure and provide light in the darkness. in more ways than one. We'd build community, offer resources, and fight not only for our son, but for the Usher syndrome community at large. I glanced around the room at the wide-eyed faces of our little community and smiled. They were finally able to understand what we were going through, and now, they knew exactly what they could do to help.

In the days after the event, calls and texts continued to stream in. Our friends and family were so proud; they, too, felt galvanized to help find a cure. We sent people to our donation page in droves and donations poured in faster than we'd ever imagined. Yet, as the weeks and months wore on, the calls and texts slowed. Once hourly, the calls now came daily and then weekly, if that. The world went back to business as usual while our little family was stuck in the throes of learning to live with Usher syndrome.

Until then, we'd spent so much time focusing on the future that we never stopped to let ourselves grieve. Now, with our first event behind us, we began to realize that we were once again isolated with very few connections outside of the medical community. The boys continued to attend a mainstream private school in Seattle, so we weren't surrounded by families who had much experience with disabilities, let alone anything as insidious as Usher. Of course, we loved our friends at Listen & Talk, but we couldn't deny how different our struggle had become than anything they ever encountered. Once again, we were back on our little island, praying that the funds we raised would help researchers make headway, and soon.

As the days lengthened and the sun soaked the earth, the end of the school year was swiftly approaching. One Friday afternoon, Conner and Cole both came home with bright blue invitations in hand—Marshall, a little boy in their class, was having a birthday party that weekend.

Holding the invites in my hands, I felt a swell of excitement. Cole had always had an easy time making friends, but Conner had often struggled. It was hard for kids his age to understand his unique rhythm, and it was easier for them to ignore him than try. But now, with more information about our foundation spreading, I wondered whether the tide was turning. I promised the kids that we'd go and made plans to scoop up a gift in the morning on the way.

The boys chattered excitedly about the party for the rest of the evening and got up and ready to go hours before it was set to start. Rubbing my eyes, I lowered myself to the floor and played cars with them, went through Conner's OT exercises, and packed us up when it was time. I soon found myself crossing the plush lawn of a sprawling, white house, making my way around to the backyard with the boys in tow.

"Can I get you a drink?" Marshall's mom asked as I placed the gift on a table stacked with colorfully wrapped gifts, side by side.

"No thanks, I'm fine," I responded, distracted by Conner and Cole running out onto the lawn. I pushed my hands into my pockets and fiddled with my purse as a familiar wave of anxiety overcame me. I hated being in social settings with people I didn't know. I felt like I didn't know where to stand, what to do with my hands, or how to hold myself at all. I willed myself to take deep breaths. I couldn't feign a headache or a family emergency; I had to do this for my boys.

I waved to a group of moms who sat around the patio table, each sipping diet sodas and water from sweating bottles. Conner and Cole wasted no time joining in the fun, grabbing Nerf guns off the grass and bolting toward the swing set. I paid careful attention as Cole joined the group of boys and Conner busied himself figuring out how the Nerf gun worked, bringing it closer to his face to see its small parts. He fumbled with the trigger, pulled the dart out, and scrunched his face as he tried to push it back in. As badly as I wanted to go and help him, I forced myself to stay put. He had to figure it out for himself, and I knew he would.

"Come sit with us!" Marshall's mom called. I headed toward the one empty seat at the table, which was painfully close to the others. I clumsily sat down as the women continued to talk.

"The thing is, I get it, I do," a blonde woman said. "These kids need structure, but having lunch so late in the afternoon can't be good for them."

"You're exactly right," another woman said. "I say they need fewer snacks and more time for real meals."

"Right? What do you think about all this, Lane? Isn't it absurd to have them wait that long to eat?" Marshall's mom asked.

I swallowed hard. I wanted to be a part of the conversation, but I genuinely had nothing to say. I wasn't worried about what time my boys were having lunch. I was concerned about whether Conner was in the right place at all. Was the curriculum right for him? Was he able to make it through the day without a blow-up? Did people understand his disabilities? Were people kind? Were any of his classmates playing with him? I quickly drew a breath and nodded.

"I agree," I said. "12:30 is a late lunch for kids their age."

As the women continued to talk, I looked over at Conner, who was now sitting on the ground watching the other kids play. Cole hopped off the slide and ran over, trying to get him to join in, but Conner shook his head and stayed still. I looked at a group of boys excitedly playing a game of war, volleying shots back and forth as they laughed and nudged one another. Conner remained on the lawn.

"I'm so glad you came," Marshall's mom chirped. "Conner seems to be enjoying himself. Gosh, by the way—we heard what's been happening with him. We're just so sorry."

I looked around the table as the moms nodded in unison, their eyebrows scrunched, their eyes sad. I felt my heart rate pick up and my entire body stiffen. I didn't know what to say. No words were coming. I somehow managed, "Thanks."

That's when a sense of dread washed over me: We weren't invited to the party because anyone really wanted us there. We were invited because it was the "nice" thing to do. I looked around the table as the women slowly went back to their conversation. They were all beautifully made up and casually dressed in that way that was intentional but looked effortless. I glanced down at myself; my jeans hadn't fit perfectly since yo-yoing of my post-pregnancy weight. My hair hung limp at my shoulders, and I hadn't worn makeup in days. In that moment, I began to realize that a chasm was growing between "us" and "them." Our lives had become about dealing with challenges, working for a cure, and finding ways to survive. I'd never know a life as straightforward as theirs. I'd never know the luxury of worrying about *normal* things. We'd never be like everyone else. We'd always be different.

I pushed my chair away from the table, mumbling an excuse. I jogged across the lawn and sat next to Conner, placing my hand on his back.

"Want to go home, buddy?" I asked.

He answered with a quiet nod. I stood up, took his hand, and called out for Cole, who was eating three Pixy Stix at the top of the slide. He waved a quick goodbye, slid down the slide, and crossed the lawn to join us as we headed to the car.

Fourteen

CONNER KICKED AT HIS Star Wars sheets as he slowly opened his eyes and smiled wide. Perched at the end of his bed, I leaned forward and squeezed his hand. His head was still wrapped in gauze and bandages, his right ear covered with the now-familiar white plastic dome. Just that morning, at the age of seven, he'd made it through his second cochlear implant surgery with flying colors; we were even able to be discharged a couple hours after surgery so Conner could recover in his own bed. This was especially exciting, because Conner was all sunshine and smiles. The nurses swooned over him as we packed our things, deliriously excited that he would soon be able to hear with both ears.

After his first surgery several years prior, the doctors decided not to place bilateral cochlear implants, because they wanted to preserve any remaining hair cells for future attempts to restore his hearing. However, now that Conner had an Usher syndrome diagnosis, we had other things to worry about, such as his safety. It was important that he could localize sound so he could listen for danger, like cars coming when he crossed the street. As a result, he needed all the hearing he could get.

I drew a breath as Conner rubbed his eyes and slowly remembered that the dome was in place. He fidgeted as I sat with my hand resting on my belly. I was pregnant again with another little boy: Hunter. Although life was crazy, Todd and I were determined to make it work. The new pregnancy would be a good thing to focus on—new life, endless joy. I had to admit that this pregnancy was coming with challenges I never expected. Though I was doing incredibly well physically, mentally, I was finding things hard. With two pregnancies under my belt, I'd become used to friends and family excitedly hearing the news that we were expecting. I loved their big, exuberant squeals, the thrill of talking about my cravings, and the joy of sharing our short list of names. Yet now, when I told people I was pregnant, I saw something heartbreaking in their eyes: concern. If I wasn't certain how they felt about our situation before I became pregnant, I was doubly sure now. People thought our situation with Conner was so awful that they wondered why we'd want to risk doing it all over again. It made my heart ache.

Now wide awake, Conner pushed himself out of bed and ran into the living room.

"Slow down," I called as I shuffled behind him. He planted himself on the couch and handed me the remote. Smiling weakly, I flipped the TV to his favorite show and placed a blanket over him.

I jogged into the kitchen as my phone began to ring. I frowned at the caller ID, which showed a number from Massachusetts. My brow scrunched, I answered.

"This is Lane."

"Hi, Lane, my name is Mark Dunning. Researchers at Boys Town gave me your number. I hope it's okay that I'm calling."

"Of course. It's nice to meet you."

"Likewise—you have no idea. My daughter was recently diagnosed with Usher syndrome. I believe she's around the same age as your son, Conner. We've been struggling with, well, everything. We didn't know where to turn, and the geneticist pointed me in your direction. I found your number on the Hear See Hope website; I hope it's okay that I called."

"It's more than okay," I replied finally. "I know exactly what you're going through, Mark. You are not alone. How can we help?"

I put Mark on speakerphone, and Todd and I spent the next hour on the phone listening to his daughter's story, taking in their unique struggle with Usher syndrome, and navigating a landscape of questions without answers. His story was so similar to ours I could hardly believe it. Mark told me that he and his wife Julia lived in Boston, which was ironic, because Todd and I had plans to be in Boston a couple of weeks later to support Todd's brother at a big movie premiere.

"We'd love to meet you," I said. "Just name a place and time."

"Thank you," Mark replied, his voice cracking. "Thank you so much."

Three months later, Todd and I raced up Newbury Street in a cab, which stopped in front of a beautiful restaurant called Sonsie. We paid the cab driver and hustled inside to see Mark standing by the bar.

Todd and I wrapped him in hugs and we immediately launched into conversation. Though we'd never met in person, a sense of familiarity immediately washed over all of us. We talked about Conner as a baby, the profound deafness diagnosis, the hearing aids, and the implants. We shared the story of his Usher diagnosis, the pain and anxiety, his progress in school, and the challenges we all faced. We left no stone unturned.

"I know you have the foundation up and running," Mark said. "Can I do something to help?"

"We'd love to bring you on board," Todd said eagerly. "What are your thoughts about what we can do better? Do you see areas of opportunity?"

"You're doing such an amazing thing. All I can say is that we need better connection and community—look how hard it was even for even the two of us to connect! We need answers, and we need concrete steps toward a cure."

"That's *exactly* why we built Hear See Hope," Todd said, leaning forward. "As we head into the future, we're doing our best to raise funds for research, but there's so much more we can do."

Mark took a breath and launched into sharing ideas, making suggestions, and breaking down all the ways he believed we could make a difference; I let Todd and Mark debate the logistics. As Mark spoke, my shoulders dropped. I hated what Julia and Mark were going through, but I was so relieved to finally talk with someone who understood—and I mean really *understood*—what we had been going through for so long. The evening slipped by in a sea of *me too's* and *same here's*. By the time we left the restaurant, Todd and I had made the decision to ask Mark to come on as a board member for Hear See Hope.

As I eased myself into bed, I cradled my swollen belly. With my mind still buzzing after meeting Mark, I let myself settle into the silence of the room. Todd and I didn't need words to say what we were both feeling: *Finally, we are not alone.*

Two days after we got home from Boston, I sat on the couch with my feet tucked beneath me. I was watching tiny dust particles as they danced in the lamplight of the living room as Todd came in and sat beside me.

"You okay?" he asked.

"Are we doing the right thing?" I asked

"Yes, we're doing the exact right thing. Lane, he needs to better understand what's going on with him. He needs to be able to put a name to all this."

I nodded.

"You're right, I know you are. I'm just—I'm scared."

"I know you are, but this is something we have to do," he said, rubbing my back. "Boys! Can you come in here? We need to talk to you."

Conner and Cole thundered into the room and bounced onto the loveseat across from us. Todd squeezed my hand as the boys tussled with one another, wrestling for the "best" spot on the couch. I watched

Conner as laughed, nudging Cole until he eventually hit him back. I chewed my bottom lip as Todd drew a breath, a sense of dread creeping up my spine. I was suddenly struck by the overwhelming feeling that this was the moment *before*. After this conversation, Conner's life would never be the same.

"Boys," Todd began, "we have something we need to talk to you about,"

Both boys stopped fidgeting and sat up straight, their eyes wide.

"Something bad?" Conner asked.

"Nothing bad, but it's important," I replied.

Conner knitted his eyebrows together as my heart palpitated.

"Conner, I want to talk to you about some of the challenges you've been facing," Todd said. "I know that you understand what your cochlear implants are for—"

"Right, I'm deaf," he responded.

"That's right, but I wanted to talk a little bit about what else is going on—with your vision, I mean."

"I have glasses because I can't see well," he said. "I don't get why we need to talk about this. I already know all this stuff."

"Right, but it's a little more complicated than deafness and blurry vision. You have something called Usher syndrome. It's a rare genetic disease that impacts vision and hearing."

I drew a breath.

"Buddy, the disease is *progressive*," I said. "That means it can get worse over time. We want you to know so you have a name for what's been going on. We want to help you understand."

"Are you okay, buddy?" Todd asked.

Conner nodded.

"Yes."

"This is why we started the foundation we've been working on," I continued. "Hear See Hope isn't just for people dealing with deafness. It's for people with Usher syndrome, like you. We're working toward a cure, and we're hopeful that we'll have it within the next ten years."

"Exactly," Todd added. "Buddy, we're working so hard to find a cure. We're hopeful that we'll find answers before your vision gets worse. Until then, we're doing everything we can to get you in the right place for school. Some people just don't understand."

My eyes fell on Cole, whose face was scrunched. He looked down at his hands and started picking at his thumbnail. I leaned forward.

"Cole, what are you feeling right now?" I asked.

"I guess now I know why things have been this way," Cole said, pressing his lips together.

"What do you mean?" Todd asked.

"I just mean that I have to take care of Conner a lot," he said with tears forming. "I keep having to move from school to school, I have to—"

I stood, crossed the room, and sat between Conner and Cole on the loveseat. I placed my arm around him.

"We see how much you do for him, Cole," I said. "And we love you so much."

"I know," he said, wiping a tear from his cheek. As he took a deep breath and calmed himself, I saw something in him I hadn't yet recognized. There, as he steeled himself, I saw pieces of myself in my son. Sometimes, things are hard. And sometimes, we have to push through.

A LONG, SPINDLY BRANCH grazed the windowpane of my bedroom, its last remaining leaves fluttering in the breeze. With my belly big and bulbous, I wrestled with a small flat box, tugging at a brand new blue mobile and untangling its strings. Just then, two sets of little footsteps thundered down the hallway and Cole and Conner burst into the room.

"Conner stole my truck!" Cole yelled, his cheeks flushing red.

"No, no, no!" Conner said, shaking his head aggressively.

I took a deep breath.

"Boys," I said softly, "let's calm down. Here, your brother is kicking. Feel."

I sat down in the plush glider and motioned for them to come close. They each placed a hand on my belly, eyes wide and giggling as the soft thumps bumped their palms.

"Is he coming today?" Cole asked, his head cocked.

"Not today, but it looks like he'll be here *tomorrow*," I responded with a grin. Though the thought of being induced scared me, I was grateful that I wouldn't have to play the guessing game this time. Things always moved so fast when I was in labor that I feared baby three would come at any moment, too fast for me to get myself to the hospital. Tomorrow was Thanksgiving, my favorite holiday. But this year, instead of eating savory turkey and spiced pumpkin pie, we'd be bringing a baby into the world.

That night, as Todd read in the lamplight, I packed last-minute items into my bag—a hairbrush, hair ties, shampoo, and a soft cotton bathrobe I'd bought just for the hospital. Once the bag was zipped and ready to go, I headed down the hallway for one last look in the nursery. Even in the low light, it looked impossibly lush and cozy. As crazy as our journey had been, being a parent was still the greatest gift in the world. Preparing for Hunter, I was getting to do all of the magical things all over again. This time, I'd carefully decorated the room in blue and khaki, curated a collection of clothes, and bought more pairs of tiny shoes than he could ever wear. I stared at the crib, lingering in anticipation of the moment when I'd lay him down there for the very first time.

When my eyes cracked open the next day, I tried to process what I was seeing. The windows were coated in a thin layer of ice, and small mounds of snow had built up in the corners. I threw off the covers and ran to the window to see at least a foot of snow on the ground and more cascading from the sky. My stomach lurched as a gust of wind howled, swirling over the lawn and kicking up a tornado of sparking flakes.

I raced into the kitchen where Todd was pushing eggs around in a pan for the boys. He looked up from the stove.

"Morning, babe!"

"How can we get to the hospital today in all this?" I asked, rubbing my eyes.

"Let's give them a call and see—maybe it'll stop later."

I ran my hands over my belly as I made my way to the table where the kids sat playing handheld video games. I kissed them each on the top of the head before dialing my doctor's office, pushing 1 for non-emergency and 2 for the nurse. I listened as the recorded message played: "We are currently closed due to severe weather. If this is an emergency, please dial 911. For all non-emergency calls, please stay on the line to leave a message for our on-call nurse."

Within the hour, I was back in bed, my back against the headboard as I stared into space. The nurse called back to let me know we had to reschedule the following day due to the weather. I'd been so excited about having Hunter on Thanksgiving that I felt real grief knowing we had to wait. As I picked at my nails, Todd poked his head into the room.

"Can I do anything?" he asked. "I know this is disappointing."

"I just...wanted to meet him today," I said.

"Me too. But tomorrow is just one sleep away, right?"

I nodded.

"You're right. We didn't get anything to make tonight. I hate to ask, but do you think you can get to the store? Just grab anything you can get. I want the boys to have a good Thanksgiving."

"Of course. You take some time to rest."

I closed my eyes as Todd put on his boots and trudged to the car. I must have slept for several hours, because I woke to the smell of turkey drifting beneath the door. I cradled my belly as I sat up, placing my feet on the floor and pulling on the robe from my suitcase. As I entered the kitchen, I almost started to cry. Todd was bent over basting a golden-brown turkey breast as green beans and potatoes bubbled on the stove. The boys were playing quietly on the living room floor as I inhaled notes of cinnamon and nutmeg. Now, the snow that had once seemed burdensome was making the house feel cozy and warm. Gratitude washed over me. If Hunter couldn't be born today, then this was exactly how I wanted to spend the holiday instead.

As the sky turned purple and the snow slowed to a stop, Todd, the boys, and I gathered around the table. We piled our plates high with turkey and stuffing, vegetables, and big, buttery rolls. Tall, pillar candles in the center of the table were dripping with wax, their flames casting playful shadows on the walls. Conner and Cole giggled with each other as Todd and I looked on, laughing with our two boys, a perfect pair. Despite our challenges, they were amazing. And now, our family was about to grow once more.

The next day, I lay in a hospital bed beneath the stiff, bleached sheets I knew so well. My contractions were beginning to pick up steam, but the pain was tolerable—thank you, epidural! Todd held my hand as the pressure swelled, kissing my head in the breaks between contractions when I let him. Todd was good like that; he knew how to read the room when I was in labor.

Soon, the doctor came to perform a check.

"It's just about time, Momma!" she said. "Just about fifteen more minutes and we'll have you push." I looked up at Todd as the doctor left again to prepare.

"Get the boys!" I said. Todd rushed into the waiting room and came back with Conner and Cole by his side, our nanny trailing behind. Sheepishly, the boys approached the bed.

"Is he here?" Cole asked.

"Yeah, where is he?" Conner chimed in, craning his neck.

"He's coming any minute," Todd replied.

I clenched my fists, breathing through a sharp contraction.

Soon, the doctor returned, flanked by two nurses. Todd settled the boys on a nearby chair as the nurses adjusted the bed. The doctor washed her hands and pulled on a pair of gloves.

"Are you ready to meet your son!?" she asked excitedly. I nodded, tearing up. I drew my knees to my sides and, on the doctor's count, began to push. I glanced at the boys, who were wide-eyed as the pressure intensified. At the team's signal, I pushed again.

"He's almost here, Lane—he's nearly out," Todd said.

I pushed again.

And again.

Then it came: a sharp cry.

I collapsed onto the bed as the nurses wiped Hunter off and set him directly on my chest. I kissed the top of his head, breathing in the sweet, earthy scent of new life. Todd slowly ushered the boys over to the bedside. Their eyes were wide, smiles big and toothy as they clutched the railings and leaned in.

"Hi, brother," Conner said, reaching out his hand.

As the doctor finished cleaning me up, Todd eased Hunter into his hands. The boys scampered to an oversized chair near the window as Todd brought Hunter over, carefully stooping down and angling him so they could see. Conner stared in awe and Cole let Hunter's fingers wrap around his pointer finger. We were now a family of five.

Once Hunter was back in my hands, my stomach tied itself into a familiar knot.

"When can we do the newborn hearing screening?" I asked the nurse.

I watched as her eyes fell on Conner. She pressed her lips together as she noticed his implants.

"Once you're settled into your room," she said, "we'll get someone to come do the test as soon as possible."

"That's fine; just make sure the audiologists know that it's urgent," Todd said, squeezing my shoulder. Just then, the doctor stood and the nurses covered my lower half with a sheet and pulled the sides of the bed up with a clank. Within the hour, an audiologist with a flippy ponytail came in with testing equipment and started attaching electrodes to Dalton.

Waves of nausea passed over me while we waited, and as Todd flipped through the channels on the TV trying to find something for the boys to watch. I did my best not to catastrophize, to stay in the moment and bask in the joy of welcoming our sweet baby boy. As scenes from *Star Wars* flitted across the screen, transfixing Conner and Cole, the nurse returned with a soft knock on the door.

"Is he okay?" I blurted.

"Yes, Mom! I'm so excited to tell you that Hunter's hearing is perfectly fine. No need to worry about anything at all."

Todd leaned over and enveloped me in a bear hug. I cried onto his shoulder as the nurse patted my leg and walked out of the room. Todd stepped over to the crib and lifted Hunter out, cradling him in his arms. Tears streamed down my cheeks as I let relief flood my body. Here we were, a family of five. I was happy.

Hunter was an amazing baby, and he slid into the family seamlessly. During my pregnancy, we had made the decision for me to leave my job and stay home with the boys, and I was now adjusting to life at home. Fully focused on my role as a mom, I quickly saw the benefits of being so hands-on. Within the first few weeks, Hunter wasn't only sleeping through the night—he was on a nap and feeding schedule that allowed me to rest, breathe, and take care of the big boys. We had help from a part-time nanny for school pickup and drop-off, so I was no longer running from place to place at breakneck speed. I was finally able to enjoy the life Todd and I had worked so hard to build. I was feeling more like *me* than I had in years. I was rested. I was confident.

Because of this, the first several months with Hunter flew by. It was a swirl of tummy time, baby giggles, and measuring milestones. Hunter was a big baby just like Conner and Cole had been. Much like Cole, he got onto his hands and knees early and was clumsily crawling by seven months. I loved watching him crawl after Conner and Cole while they rolled around roughhousing, playing silly games, and just being boys. Hunter just wanted to be a part of the gang, and he was.

Sometimes, as I sat listening to their giggles, I just knew: Our kids were such an incredible blessing. There was so much joy. I loved being a mom, and I couldn't get enough.

In fact, I wanted even more.

Sixteen

I N AUGUST OF THAT same year, Todd and I embarked on a new journey. We were trying for baby number four; this time, however, we had made the difficult decision to undergo IVF, a procedure in which my egg would be fertilized in a laboratory and implanted into my uterus. Despite the fact that Conner was doing so well, we knew we didn't want to risk who had Usher syndrome if we could help it. Todd and I spent hours weighing our options. Should we toss our desire for a big family aside because of the risks? Should we accept that what we had was good enough and simply move forward? Or was there a better way?

Having looked at it from every angle, Todd and I decided to look into pre-implantation genetic diagnosis (PGD). Although fertility treatments were relatively new, we'd come to understand that when going through IVF, which was a necessary part of PGD, our embryos would go through genetic testing for Usher syndrome. This meant that we'd be able to intentionally select the embryo that had the highest chance of not having it. To us, this provided us with the ability to grow our family without the risk of having a child who would need to overcome genetic abnormalities.

Over the next several months, I braved hormones, needles, and egg retrievals. We held our breath waiting for a call from the geneticist, worried that all of our embryos would show markers of Usher syndrome. When we finally received the call, we were elated: We'd made several embryos that were free of any genetic abnormalities. Soon after, I was implanted with a perfect embryo. Then, it was time to wait.

Although Todd and I were jumping for joy, we kept our excitement between the two of us. Considering all we had going on, our families had already given us a hard time about choosing to have a third baby. Now that we'd made the decision to have a fourth, things had reached a fever pitch, and no one seemed to share in our elation. Anytime we told anyone the news, I braced myself for the feigned excitement and wide, concerned eyes. It was as if having a child with special needs precluded us from the joy of growing our family: Since things were already *so bad*, why would we even *consider* something that could make it *worse*?

In spite of the connections we'd made through all the things we'd been through, I still felt like I was on an island sometimes, desperate for connection. I often sat quietly rocking Hunter in the glider, wishing that I had someone—anyone—aside from Todd to excitedly talk with about this next phase of our family's great adventure.

As my belly grew, I felt like Supermom. Conner was now nine years old, Cole was seven, and Hunter was nine months. Though tired, I was nailing life as a mom of three. I was moving through life in a well-choreographed dance, balancing schedules, nap times, feeding times, activities, and homework sessions.

As summer drew to a close, I once again started the search for a new school. We'd seen private schools, Catholic schools, and, of course, our nearby public schools. Conner was being put through interviews and testing, all of which proved nearly impossible for him. My heart sank whenever I watched him in these settings, across from frustrated teachers or administrators talking him through the exam. His cheeks would turn pink, his eyes red as he choked back tears. I couldn't understand why people were so hard-hearted, so unwilling to understand what made Conner tick. This wasn't what I wanted for him—not by a long shot.

We soon decided to settle ourselves into public school. Thanks to our individualized education plan, Conner was given support for hearing and vision, and would be set up with an FM device in his classrooms so he could hear the teacher through an earpiece, helping him to have better communication access in a loud classroom. Though things started off well, they soon became bumpy. Conner struggled to see the board and had issues keeping up, and his class sizes were very large. Seeing him struggle shattered my heart. Conner deserved better, and we wouldn't stop until we figured out exactly where he could get it.

One sunny June afternoon, I stood slowly from my rocker with Hunter on my hip. Conner and Cole had been doing activities outside with the nanny while I gave Hunter a bottle and got him settled for a nap. I placed him in the crib and reached to pull the curtains closed when I felt a familiar tightening sensation. I stopped and stood in a slash of sunlight. There it was: a contraction. I waddled into the living room, grabbed my phone, and dialed Todd.

"Is it time?" he asked.

"Yes, come home!" I replied.

Knowing how efficient my body was at birthing babies, Todd raced home and scooped me up right away. We were barely at the hospital for an hour before the anesthesiologist had me leaning over a pillow as he inserted the epidural. I squeezed Todd's hands until they were purple, gritting my teeth through the discomfort. Once the doctor finished, the nurses helped me into bed not a moment too soon since my contractions were coming fast. But there was a problem: I could still feel every bit of the pain. There was no relief from the epidural—*zero*. I grabbed Todd's shirt, balling it in my fist as I pulled him toward me.

"Get the doctor. I need another epidural—*NOW!*"

Todd raced out of the room and came back with a blond nurse in pink scrubs who leaned into me.

"I'm sorry, Mom," she said gently. "It's too late to give you another."

I wanted to punch her in the face.

The pain crashed over me and swept me under like a rogue wave beating the shore. I clawed at the sheets, let out primal screams, and pinched my eyes shut until my head pounded. I felt the ripping sensation of Dalton coming down, then the tearing as he slid out of my body. He let out a cry as the nurse placed him on my chest, and I let out a heaving sob.

"It's good to see you, buddy," Todd said, a tear sliding down his cheek. He brushed the hair from my face as I sobbed and whispered, "I'm so proud of you, Lane."

I softly maneuvered Dalton into my arms so I could look at his sweet face. His dark eyes opened for a moment as he scanned my face before wrinkling his own into a grimace. I ran my fingers over his ears and noticed something on each one. I tried to brush them away, to pick them off like pieces of fuzz, but they stayed firmly in place. They were skin tags. My stomach fell, and my heart slammed against my ribs.

"Todd, look." He narrowed his eyes and leaned in. In a panic, I waved a nurse over and pointed to Dalton's ears.

"What are these?" I asked. "Is he okay? Is this bad?"

"Don't worry, Mom, they're just skin tags—nothing to be concerned about."

"But this can indicate something really wrong, like deafness. Our oldest son is deaf—not just deaf, he has—"

"Mom," the nurse said, patting my knee, "I understand that you're upset and scared, but this isn't anything to be concerned about. We'll get you out of here shortly, and then we'll get him a thorough check-up. But he looks fantastic. Look at those cheeks!"

I looked up at Todd, whose brow was furrowed. I knew exactly what he was thinking, because I was thinking it too. Skin tags indicated something—we'd learned about it in one of our many sessions with Conner. I could feel myself becoming hysterical, and knew we needed the hearing screening as soon as humanly possible. I tried to calm my nerves by thinking about the IVF process. We'd run every test imaginable and received great news every step of the way. Dalton was healthy—wasn't he?

I felt ready to crawl out of my skin as I watched the nurses move at a snail's pace around my room, writing schedules on the whiteboard and putting postpartum care items in the bathroom. When they finally left, I stared at Todd with desperate eyes.

"I know I'm being crazy, but I'm just so scared," I said.

"I know," he replied. "I am too."

I was fighting back tears.

"It's okay, Mom," one of the nurses said as she lifted Dalton off my chest. "There's nothing to worry about."

I nodded, chewing the inside of my cheeks as she placed Dalton in the crib with the clear sides and swaddled him. I looked at Todd for reassurance, but he was sitting in a nearby chair with his head in his hands. Sensing my gaze, he looked up.

"It's going to be okay," he said, offering a forced smile.

"I know," I lied.

It seemed like the test was taking forever. Todd was pacing the floor, and I was looking at the facial expressions of the audiologist. I knew something was wrong.

"He's deaf, isn't he?" I blurted. Todd squeezed my hand.

The audiologist sat down on a chair in the corner and leaned forward, tilting a small stack of papers in our direction. We'd become so accustomed to the charts that he didn't even have to speak. There it was: the thick black line illustrating normal hearing levels and a broken line far below it indicating Dalton's results: profound deafness.

I wanted to scream. I wanted to jump from the bed and throttle the audiologist, break the windows, and claw my way out of this world and into the next. Todd sat down on the bed beside me, tears streaming down his face.

"How did this happen?" Todd asked.

"We did PGD," I said. "We tested everything and nothing came up. This can't be happening."

"I understand this is a lot to take in," the audiologist said, but I stopped listening. She had to be wrong. She didn't know what she was doing. She had no idea what she was talking about.

"Your best next step is to make an appointment at Children's for another screening, then—"

"We know," Todd finished. "Our oldest son was born profoundly deaf and has Usher syndrome."

"That's right. You'll need to hang tight for a bit until they're able to do a sedation test—they can perform one at five to six months. In the meantime, try to remember: As you well know, this is extremely hard news. But on the other side of things, Dalton is extremely healthy."

The audiologist stood as Dalton began to cry. Todd crossed the room and picked him up, bringing him to his shoulder and patting him on the back. She placed the small stack of papers on the rolling table that stretched across my bed. I stared down at the lines on the graph, wanting to tear the pages to shreds and throw them on the floor. I couldn't bear to flip through them; the last thing I wanted to see was the pamphlet of information about hearing aids with smiling children on the front.

"Take care, Mom and Dad, and congratulations—he's beautiful," the audiologist said as she breezed out of the room. Todd placed Dalton in my arms as I let the tears come. I cried for everything—for Dalton, for us, for all of the effort we'd put in to avoid this. Yet, here we were, knocked all the way back to the starting line with the sweet, beautiful baby we'd tried so hard to protect.

"I knew it," I managed. "When I saw those skin tags, I *knew*."

"The thing is though, the genetic testing didn't show Usher syndrome markers, so we know it's not that. The deafness has to be unrelated."

"But the skin tags—what if it's something even worse?""What if the skin tags are nothing at all? We know how to handle this, Lane. We've done it before, and we'll do it again."

"I know. I'm just exhausted."

"Let's get some rest. I'll handle making the appointment, just be with Dalton now. I'm going to text the family and tell them that he's here and that he's healthy. The rest can wait."

Todd kissed us both on the forehead and sat back down in the corner chair with his phone. I maneuvered Dalton into position and let him latch onto my breast, tracing his face with my finger as he worked his jaw. My heart ached at the thought of doing it all over again—the screenings, the therapies, the implants, the frustration, the pain. However, one fact kept me grounded. According to every test we'd done, Dalton didn't have Usher syndrome. At the very least, we knew that to be true.

Yet, as I ran my finger along the skin tag on his left ear, unease set in. What if they *were* something? Suddenly, the knowledge that it wasn't Usher caused a swell of panic. If it was something worse, what would we do? Sure, it could be more of the same, but it could be something entirely new. Then what? Only time would tell.

The next day, we were discharged early, so we scurried into the car and made our way directly to Children's Hospital to see Dr. Sharon, Conner's audiologist, who felt like family. We were fortunate that they were able to see us right away to perform a secondary, more in-depth newborn auditory screening. As soon as we were in the exam room, Todd and I each assumed our usual roles. He sat on a chair in the corner as I eased Dalton onto the table lined with crinkly white paper. My body still aching, I settled Dalton as the technicians prepared the probes they'd stick onto the sides of his head and the tiny headphones they'd place in his ears. By the time Dr. Sharon cracked the door, my palms were sweating.

"Lane, Todd, I am so sorry for what you're going through," Dr. Sharon said, crossing the room. "What a sweet boy. He's precious just like his brothers. Listen, we're going to get this all sorted out, okay?"

Images were racing through my mind. After we'd managed to clumsily get through the IVF process and I'd made peace with the pain, Todd and I felt unwaveringly hopeful. Now, I was staring into Dr. Sharon's sympathetic eyes, recognizing hints of pity as she placed her hand on my arm.

"I just don't know how this could have happened," I managed. "We did PGD this time, we did all the tests, we did—"

"Everything," Todd finished. "We did *everything* to avoid this."

The door opened and Dr. Kate, Dalton's otolaryngologist, took a seat.

"Hi, Todd and Lane," Dr. Kate said with a nod. "I know you didn't expect to be here, but we're here now, and we're going to clarify the results and make sure we know what we're dealing with."

"Dr. Kate, do you see these skin tags?" I asked. "What could they be? It could be something bad, right?"

"It *could* be, but the skin tags could very well be unrelated."

"But what could it be?" I begged. "Please, I need to know. Just tell me."

She drew a breath.

"Listen, Lane, I hear you. Let's get this test underway so we can begin to get some answers." Dr. Kate placed the tiny headphones in Dalton's ears and placed two probes on his head. I watched as she adjusted knobs on a nearby machine, made notes, and squinted her eyes at the screen. Dalton remained asleep, swaddled in a muslin blanket I'd packed for the hospital. My eyes fell on the skin tags. I felt sick.

Soon, Dr. Kate sat back.

"Okay, it looks like we can confirm the results of the hospital test. Our test indicates that we are in fact dealing with profound deafness in Dalton. Now, let's not jump to conclusions just yet. Let's—"

"When can we do the implant?" I blurted.

"Yes, we need to get on a list now," Todd added.

"Significant changes have taken place since Conner went through this, which will make things a bit easier this go around. They'll do the implants much younger now, closer to the six-month mark."

"Can we get it done sooner?" Todd pleaded.

"We may be able to, but the main issue is weight. Dalton is big like Conner was, so I don't think there will be a problem. I'm with you every step of the way, and we'll get this handled."

"What about the skin tags?" I asked. "What if—"

"One step at a time," she replied. "We'll get him in for bloodwork as soon as possible, then we can put your mind at ease."

Dr. Kate gently removed the headphones from Dalton's ears and the probes from his head and made her way out of the room with a compassionate goodbye. I scooped Dalton into my arms and kissed his silky forehead. As I placed him gently in his car seat and draped the muslin blanket over him, I found myself hoping for the unthinkable. At least with Usher, we'd known what we were getting ourselves into. I sat down on the hard plastic chair as Todd strapped Dalton in. It struck me that I was hoping for the very thing I'd tried to wish away so many times since Conner's diagnosis.

"Please, God," I whispered. "Let it be Usher."

As the days went on and my body began to heal, it felt as though our lives had been turned upside down. Of course, there were the phone calls from well-meaning family members who all tried to sound upbeat on the phone, but as soon as I shared any details, I could hear them reaching for something to say. All anyone managed were short, clipped responses.

I'm sorry you're dealing with this.

You're going to get through this.

I wish there was something I could do.

Despite the kindness our loved ones showed, I couldn't help but key into the undertone of every conversation I had. Despite their syrupy compassion, I knew exactly what they were thinking:

What did you think was going to happen?

You made the choice to have another one—this is your fault.

This is a consequence of your poor judgment.

With each phone call I received, the pain got a little bit worse. I'd sit with Dalton in my arms and rock him softly, wishing that he could hear my voice just once. I'd tell him that I loved him, that it would all be okay, that we would do whatever it took to give him the best life possible, and, of course, that I was sorry. I would do anything for it to be me and not Dalton, not Conner.

Despite my commitment to forging ahead, I found myself frozen in ways I'd never imagined. I was numb; I didn't want to fight anymore. With Conner, Todd and I immediately sprang into action. We focused our attention on the implants, the surgeries, the IFSP, the schooling, all of it. This time, however, things were different. I'd spent the last nine years battling at every turn to get Conner the best care possible. I'd spent all of my time climbing a mountain akin to Everest. Somehow, I'd scaled the rock face with confidence. I could see the top, and it was within reach—but now, I'd been knocked down to the base to climb it all over again. For now, all we could focus on were the implants. We knew that Dalton needed them. All we needed to do was to get Dalton to the point where he could undergo surgery. For the time being, that had to be our priority. In the meantime, however, the diagnosis was paramount.

Later, the geneticist had the entire immediate family come in for testing.

"Looking at these results, I'm glad to say that I don't see any markers of BOR, so I feel confident ruling that out. We still need to wait for the final results, but given your family history, I can say with a good deal of certainty that it is Usher syndrome we're dealing with in Dalton."

"How did this happen?" I asked.

"PGD is still in its infancy. The genetic tests they run aren't as comprehensive as we'd like them to be. That, combined with the fact that Usher syndrome is so rare and its genetic markers are still being identified, means that it was likely missed."

Todd placed his hand on my knee as I tried to get control of my emotions. I was overcome by a swirling combination of anger and relief, joy and grief. I stared at Todd through tired eyes, my entire body aching from the tension. Now that we knew, there was nothing left to do but fight to get the implants as soon as possible and find a way to forge ahead as a family of six, with two children living with the same rare genetic disorder.

The house was filled with the familiar smells of Saturday—butter and syrup, inky newspaper pages, and hot hazelnut coffee. Hunter and Dalton were both bundled up for mid-morning naps as Todd and I sat at the dining table in a beam of light flooding through the kitchen window.

"I think we just need to have this talk with them," Todd said. "There's no sense in waiting."

"Okay, call them in," I replied. Todd left to gather Conner and Cole and led them back into the kitchen. Conner's face was flushed like it gets when he's really into a video game, and Cole trailed behind him clutching a comic book. They each pulled out a chair at the table and sat down.

"What's wrong?" Cole asked.

"Nothing is *wrong*," Todd replied. "We just have something to talk to you about."

I cleared my throat.

"Boys, there's something you need to know about Dalton," I began. "He's had some health issues and—" I looked at Todd, silently begging him to step in.

"The thing is, boys," he said, "we've recently found out that Dalton has Usher syndrome like you, Conner."

Conner's eyes lit up.

"Wait, so, I'm not alone anymore?" he asked.

"You're not alone, and your little brother will need help as he grows up. You're already such an amazing big brother, and now there is so much you can teach him. He's so lucky to have you, Conner—and you too, Cole. Dalton is so lucky to have you, but so is Hunter. You'll teach him all the ways your kindness has made life easier for Conner."

I felt sick as a tear slid down Cole's face. It was only then that I realized the full impact of all our family had endured. Conner's Usher syndrome diagnosis meant that Cole had been forced to sacrifice so much to protect Conner from life's ups and downs. Now, he was about to watch Hunter fill the same role for Dalton. In that moment, I saw hurt in Cole's eyes that I had never fully noticed before. From little things like helping Conner walk without tripping, staving off bullies, and turning on extra lights in a room before Conner stepped inside, Cole was an expert caretaker. I stared at Cole as he cast his eyes downward, trying to process what we were saying. "How do you feel about Dalton's diagnosis, Conner?" Todd asked. "What does it mean to you?"

"It means that I'm not alone," he repeated with a smile.

"Why are you happy?" Cole asked, his forehead creasing. "This means Dalton won't be able to see or hear, either."

Conner shrugged.

"I can see and hear a little bit. I'm just different than everyone else. Now, me *and* Dalton are different than everyone else!"

"But he's going to struggle with lots of things," Cole said. "I don't think it's a good thing." He shook his head and retreated inside himself. Conner fidgeted in his chair, oblivious to Cole's point. Finally, Cole asked: "Can we go now?"

I nodded.

As the boys wandered out of the room, I slumped back in my chair. My entire body was exhausted; my back ached, my head pounded. I couldn't believe we were back in this place *again*. I couldn't shake the look on Cole's face. I found myself racked with guilt—how did this happen? How could I have worked so hard to prevent this only to end up back in the throes of it all? An action-oriented person, I was always moving forward and rarely stopped to think about the negative parts of our situation. Now, with two children living with the same rare genetic disease, I felt something I'd never expected to feel: the edges of hopelessness.

Just as I felt tears coming, Conner leapt back into the living room. He took one look at me and knew that I wasn't okay—not by a long shot. He sat down next to me and placed his head on my shoulder.

"What's wrong?" he asked.

"Nothing, I think I'm just emotional," I replied. "I'm scared about Dalton. I'm nervous that he—"

"Mom, don't be nervous. I'm happy, and Dalton will be too."

"I know, I really do."

"There's a reason this is happening. I don't understand what that is, but there's no sense living and wishing things were different."

I stared back at Conner in disbelief. He was just 10 years old, yet here he was, sharing wisdom far beyond his years. At that moment, I realized that I didn't need to view this as something to fear. Conner was thriving, and Dalton would too. After all, this really was just more of the same. We'd forged a path paved with the best doctors, case workers, specialists, surgeons, and geneticists.

Now, all we had to do was walk the path with our four boys by our side.

Seventeen

"**C**ONNER, GET DOWN HERE!" I called, pouring cereal into a bowl. The doorbell whistled its rhythmic tune.

"One minute!" Conner answered from the top of the stairs.

"Not one minute! *Now*! Your instructor's at the door!" I turned to Hunter, who was sitting

at the kitchen counter with a toaster waffle in one hand and his iPad in the other. "Could you do me a favor and let him in?"

He shook his head, eyes fixed on the screen.

"If I pause the game now, I'll lose!" he said. Sighing, I sloshed milk into the cereal bowl, pushed it across the counter, and grabbed a dish towel to wipe my hands. It had been a busy week, as usual, and now we had yet another thing to throw into the chaos we called our "routine." Over the past few months, we began to realize that Conner's vision was worsening. Despite the fact that we were continuing to work with his doctors to improve things as best we could, it was becoming clear we needed to take further action. As part of his IEP, the school provided orientation mobility services to teach him how to navigate the world by using a white cane.

The idea of the white cane was tough for me to process. Up to that point, Conner could get through life without anyone noticing that he had real issues with his vision. Sure, he wore thick glasses, but no one viewed him as blind in that way. The introduction of the white cane came with such a stigma, and I struggled to settle into the idea of him presenting as a blind boy to the world. Still, it was something I needed to get behind if I hoped to give Conner the independence he craved.

Conner had completed a few training sessions at school, which he had said very little about; today would be the first time the instructor came to our house to get him some practice in our neighborhood. I swallowed hard at the thought of our neighbors seeing him walking while tapping the cane in front of him. Pasting a smile on my face, I unbolted the door and opened it wide.

"Hi!" I said. "Mr. Bennett, is it? Great to meet you."

"Good morning, Mrs. McKittrick," the instructor replied, his eyes crinkling cheerfully. "How are you doing?"

"Good! Conner's on his way down. Do you want to step inside?"

Mr. Bennett raised his hand to decline just as Conner thundered down the stairs, sliding his hand across the banister.

"Hey!" he said.

"Hey, Conner—are you ready?" Mr. Bennett asked.

"Do everything he says," I instructed, hugging Conner before he headed out. "And be safe!" He grunted in response, darting out the door.

I remained standing in the doorway as Mr. Bennett followed Conner to the driveway, giving him an unfolded cane that measured from the floor to Conner's armpit. It had a black rubber handle at the top and a red band at the bottom, just above the rolling ball tip. Conner waved it over the concrete and I imagined the sensations in his arm: the vibration of the rough surface, minor jolts when he went over jagged rocks, and hard stops when he bumped into immovable objects, like the edge of the sidewalk. I tossed the dish towel I was still holding onto the table and slipped my feet into a random pair of sneakers, not bothering to tie the laces. Keeping a good distance from Conner and his instructor to avoid being a distraction, I followed them to the edge of the property.

They wandered through the neighborhood, Conner wearing thick goggles to simulate further vision loss. Sometimes, Mr. Bennett would hold Conner's arm, guiding him around streetlamps and fallen branches from the trees that lined the sidewalk; other times, Mr. Bennett would step back and let Conner feel for those things on his own. I swallowed the painful lump rising in my throat. Would he really need to rely on the cane one day? Would his vision really get that bad?

A family who lived a few doors down from us approached him on the sidewalk. Their children—a girl and a boy, who were in the same grade as Hunter—hid behind their parents. The mother and father looked on with a mixture of pity and confusion. My expression hardened, knowing what they were thinking. They were wondering why Conner needed a cane when they'd seen him reading from his phone screen. Maybe they considered themselves lucky to have two sighted children. Each parent grabbed one of their children's hands and parted to let Conner and his instructor pass. I was reminded of the moment when

Moses raises his staff as Conner waved his white cane, to part the red sea (in this case, a crowd of neighbors). A dog walker in a green jacket, who had been behind them, crossed the street. Then, Conner slowed to a halt.

"What's up?" I heard Mr. Bennett ask. "Do you want to stop for a minute?"

Conner shook his head, and they continued their route. His cane went *tap, tap, tap* on the sidewalk as they rounded the corner. I trudged back inside, wondering if Conner found the experience as foreign and isolating as I perceived it to be.

In the weeks that followed, Mr. Bennett introduced me to the role of a "sighted guide." I'd mistakenly believed that his instruction would be all about teaching Conner independence, but Conner was just as keen to get me involved as Mr. Bennett was. I carved out half an hour of my week to practice with them.

"Okay," Mr. Bennett said, "Now, Conner, you're going to hold your mom's upper arm, just like we practiced."

He gripped the spot just above my elbow, fingertips digging into my skin.

"What do I do?" I asked, extending my free hand.

"Nothing at all," Mr. Bennett said. "Just keep the arm he's holding by your side."

"That's it?" I let my arms go limp.

"Well, I'm going to teach you the guiding technique. It can be tempting to drag him where he needs to be, but you need to be gentle."

"Guide gently," I agreed.

"Exactly."

"I should *always* be in control," Conner added, grinning.

"Except for when it comes to choosing dessert portions," I laughed.

"Okay, shall we give it a try?" Mr. Bennett asked.

We circled the kitchen and living room, practicing the gentle guiding technique while Mr. Bennett taught me what to look out for, such as steps, changes in terrain, and sudden inclines. That afternoon, after waving goodbye to Mr. Bennett, I took the boys to Costco, and Conner and I gave the guiding technique a try. The smell of pepperoni pizza wafted over us as I placed Hunter into the cart and pushed it with one hand. Conner wrapped his ram around mine as we made our way through the bustling store. In the chaos, I dodged a man with a stroller and ran Conner into a metal shelf.

"Mom!" Conner whined.

"Sorry," I mumbled, trying to keep a hold of Conner and push the shopping cart at the same time, almost immediately walking him into a wet floor sign. He bumped into the side of it, sending it toppling over with a loud clatter.

"Mom!"

"I know, I'm trying," I said apologetically, pausing next to a shelf and bumping a crate of juice boxes into my cart. It didn't take long for my upper arm to start aching from Conner's tight grip, and by the time I'd finished shopping and piled the kids back into the car, I collapsed into the front seat and closed my eyes, physically drained.

As challenging as being a sighted guide was, I understood its importance. The alternative was letting Conner go off by himself, which could lead to him missing social cues, such as accidently cutting a line or walking in front of shoppers as they perused the shelves. Even with his cane, people might misunderstand and shout something like, "Hey! Out of the way!" As a sixth grader, he wasn't equipped to deal with that.

Getting to school was equally challenging. The crossing to the school gate didn't beep or vibrate when Conner pressed the button, and he confided in me that he couldn't always see when it was safe to cross. I dialed his orientation and mobility instructor when he was at school to explain the situation, hoping that we could brainstorm a solution.

"The local government installs those crossings, so I'm not sure what we can do to fix that, unfortunately," he said.

"I understand that," I replied patiently, "but clearly this is a dangerous situation, so we need to come up with something."

"It's more challenging to teach street crossings for Conner because it's hard for him to localize sound, due to his hearing loss. So, okay: What if we created a sign?"

"A stop sign? That could work!" I replied, hopefully.

"No," she said. "A sign for Conner to hold."

I paused, fiddling with a stray pen lid on the kitchen table.

"What do you mean?"

"Something he can hold that says, 'I'm blind, please help me cross the road.'"

I envisioned Conner standing at the edge of the sidewalk, alone, waiting for someone kind enough to stop and help him. What if they avoided him like they did when he was using his cane on the sidewalk and he got stuck there? What if a stranger with bad intentions preyed on his vulnerability? A bitter taste filled my mouth.

"That sounds... humiliating," I said finally.

"It's the best we can do for now. I can try to brainstorm a better solution with my peers," the orientation and mobility instructor said apologetically.

"This is hopeless," I murmured.

"It's not hopeless," he replied. "He'll just need to be accompanied to the gate."

I thanked her flatly and hung up. Conner had to rely on others to stay safe, all because the world wouldn't accommodate him. I felt sick.

After months of calling the school to insist that Conner's vision was worsening and he needed classroom accommodations, we eventually received news that we had been listened to. One Thursday afternoon, a vision teacher took Conner out of his English class to provide him with a box of various tools to help with accessibility. It included a magnifier and a CCTV, a huge contraption from the '70s which was nearly as big, and certainly heavier, than Conner was. The man talked him through how to set up and use the equipment's various functions, then left Conner to figure out the rest.

When I picked Conner up a couple of days later, he tossed his bag into the backseat and got in the car, sighing. I eyed his exhausted expression in the rearview mirror.

"Hey! Did you have a good day?" I asked, forcing a cheerful tone.

He shrugged.

"What's up?" I said, twisting my neck to look at him over my right shoulder.

"The CCTV," he said grumpily.

"Is it not helping?"

"I have to sit in the back corner of the classroom so it can be plugged in with a light, and it takes up *all* the room on my desk," he sulked.

"Can't you move it aside?"

"I do that, but then I have to move it back when I need it. The things I have to do to get it all set up are really hard."

I frowned.

"The teachers aren't helping you with that?"

"No, they just keep teaching," he said, sighing again. "By the time I get it ready, they start talking about something else, and I can't learn anything."

I couldn't believe what I was hearing—all of that equipment and no support? I didn't fight so hard for accommodations just to have my son stuck in a corner alone and forgotten. These tools were designed to help him, but they were doing more harm than good.

"It's overwhelming, huh, buddy?"

He nodded, forehead crinkling.

"My vision teacher even said I should learn *braille*."

I swallowed a gasp before it burst from my lips. Braille?

"But I love reading, and I *can* see—I just need a bigger font!"

"Of course you can," I replied reassuringly, trying to process the idea. First, the cane and now this. It didn't seem real. Logically, I knew that Conner's eyesight was deteriorating, but it had never felt as scary as it did now. Conner's love of reading was as ingrained in him as it had been for me at his age. Braille was obviously useful, but it wouldn't be the same—and what if he wanted to read something that hadn't been translated yet? There were other options like text to speech and audiobooks, but none of that held a candle to holding a book in your hands.

"Maybe your teacher is right," I suggested. "Maybe we should explore that option."

Later that week, after talking to Conner's IEP team, we got him started on lessons with the vision teacher from the school district. It was immediately obvious that he hated them. Sitting in an empty classroom after his friends had gone home and reading out letters as he traced their shapes on the page was as boring as it sounds. On top of that, the braille maker was a typewriter-like machine that he had no interest in learning to use. He complained relentlessly and, eventually, after he came home crying one day, we decided that large print would have to be enough.

Eighteen

F OUR WEEKS LATER, WE were still awaiting the final results of our genetic testing. The anxiety was so bad that I found myself on auto-pilot, navigating life's twists and turns with an ever-present lump in my throat. I was numb; no tears came. The pain was insurmountable. I had built a huge wall between me and the rest of the world. Of course, Todd and I knew what the tests would reveal, but it didn't help. Hearing the words would make it undeniable.

In all this, I'd somehow managed to develop and maintain a schedule for the children. I was moving through most days as easily as one can while juggling four young boys. It was amazing to see the way our family had taken shape—Conner and Cole were like a unit, always together, happily helping with the young ones, grabbing me water, and handing me diapers. Then, there were Hunter and Dalton, nearly the same distance apart as Conner and Cole, always together and bonding. In my happiest moments, I'd look around the living room at them and feel a swell of gratitude for getting to do the best parts of parenthood all over again. Yet, it was bittersweet—we'd have to repeat the bad, too.

One Tuesday afternoon, I sat in my swivel chair in my office working on a proposal when my phone pinged. I finished typing the sentence I was working on before checking it—it was an email from Conner and Cole's school.

Dear Mrs. McKittrick,

My name is Mr. Kipp, and I'm Conner's teacher. I have some troubling news for you. As you may know, we have been working hard on our math skills this year. We've been taking weekly tests on multiplication, long division, et cetera. Once the students complete these tests, I review the answers aloud, and the students grade themselves. They then hand their graded papers to me, and I perform a double check. Generally, it's a system that works quite well. However, today I caught Conner taking advantage of this situation. When I checked his work, he had marked everything correct, yet when I looked closely, he had missed approximately 60% of the answers. I'm saying that I believe Conner is cheating.

I had barely finished reading the email before smashing the reply button and typing a hasty response. I had very little patience these days, especially when it came to the boys.

Dear Mr. Kipp,

Thank you for your email expressing your concerns about Conner's recent test. With all due respect, Conner isn't the type to do something like this. He's honest to a fault and would never consciously cheat; there has to be an explanation. Are you sure he can hear you properly?

While I waited for a reply, I wiggled my mouse and stared at the blinking cursor, but all I could think about was Conner. Just when I thought the IEP was working smoothly, yet another issue arose. When would the teachers ever adjust to having a boy with Usher syndrome in their class? Mr. Kipp's response came five minutes later.

Yes, I'm sure he can hear me. We have his FM system set up; his disability is not an excuse for this, Mrs. McKittrick. Just a reminder, cheating will not be tolerated. No matter the circumstance, it is unacceptable. We're going to put him on a probationary period, monitoring him very closely. But another offense could lead us to take more serious action.

I logged out of my work computer and left a few minutes early to join Todd and the boys at home, texting Todd and biting my lip throughout the entire journey. I needed to find out from Conner what was really going on, without accusing him like Mr. Kipp had done. There was no way he had really cheated. No way.

When I stepped into the house, I went into the kitchen where Conner and Cole were putting the finishing touches on the worksheets they'd brought home from school. Conner had his head leaned close to the paper the way he always did when he was concentrating hard. I sat down at the table.

"Conner, I just spoke to Mr. Kipp. Can I ask you something?"

Conner's face flushed as he looked up at me and put his pencil down.

"Mr. Kipp says that he noticed your self-graded paper wasn't graded properly. Do you know about that?"

He shook his head.

"When you're grading your own paper, you listen to the teacher and mark anything wrong that you missed—you know that, right?"

"Yes," he said, picking at his paper.

"Mr. Kipp says you marked a lot of things right on your test that were actually wrong. What happened there? Are you having trouble hearing?"

"Yes, I can't—" a tear rolled down his flushed cheek. "The classroom is so loud, my teacher's voice is so soft, and sometimes the volume on my FM system won't go high enough for me to be able to hear over the noise. I used to ask Mr. Kipp to repeat himself, but I'd have to ask him several times. He would always get so upset with me because I was slowing the class down, and I wanted to be respectful, so I just stopped asking him. I'm good at math, and a lot of my answers *are* right, so when I can't hear, I just mark my answer as correct."

"So, you're guessing? Is that right?"

He nodded.

"Is the FM system working at all? Are you having problems all the time?"

As I watched Conner try to answer, his breath was catching so much he couldn't get the words out. The gist of what he was saying was that he was struggling to hear anything Mr. Kipp said in the classroom. Instead of stopping to help him, Mr. Kipp was chastising Conner. This meant Conner was falling behind; he couldn't keep up because he couldn't *hear*. I placed Hunter on the floor with a set of pots and pans to bang, kissed Conner on the head, and wrapped my arms around him.

"I'm going to get this sorted out, okay?" He didn't answer but hugged me back; his tears soaked through the front of my shirt. I called the school back, this time asking for the principal. I was seething by the time she returned my call.

"I do understand your predicament, Mrs. McKittrick," she said. "The issue for us, however, is that we cannot make exceptions to our rules.

Mr. Kipp is correct; this behavior is unacceptable." I tried to calm my rage, but I was incensed.

"This is absolutely shocking," I managed. "We're finished with your school. Do you hear me? We'll be there to gather Conner's things tomorrow."

"Mrs. McKittrick, I—"

"No. This conversation is over."

I kept the boys home the next day, and at 4 p.m. once all of the children had been sent home, I brought Conner to the school. I was immediately hit with the familiar scent of pencil shavings and glue sticks as we made our way down the hallway to his classroom. I drew a breath as we entered the room, its walls covered in posters, charts, and small pieces of art. Mr. Kipp sat at his desk grading papers. He looked up and quickly cast his eyes downward—he didn't bother to greet us.

I stood with Dalton's car seat in the crook of my arm, helping when possible as Conner packed all of his things into his backpack. As he stooped down and gathered papers, pencils, rulers, and packs of crayons, the magnet slipped off the side of his head and dangled to his shoulders. He quickly adjusted the earpiece and slipped the magnet back onto his head. I stared at Mr. Kipp who refused to acknowledge us; he simply sighed audibly and glanced at his watch.

Once Conner gathered the rest of his things, we made our way back into the hallway. I wanted to slam the door behind me, but I managed to get out of there without making a scene. Conner walked a few paces ahead of me, his heavy backpack over one shoulder. My heart ached. We would never set foot in this school again.

We crossed the parking lot and headed toward the car. Conner got settled in the back seat as I clicked Dalton's car seat into place. I slid into my seat behind the steering wheel, drove out of the parking lot, and turned right onto the busy road. Gripping the wheel so tightly my knuckles were white, I glanced into the rearview mirror to see Conner staring out the window. His cheeks were red, eyes swollen. All I could think about was Mr. Kipp and all the things I'd wished I'd had the wherewithal to say to him as Conner packed his desk.

It never ceased to amaze me that people could be so cold. Before we brought Conner into this world, I had a rosy view of the way life looked for those with disabilities. Of course, back then, I didn't think about it much—but whenever I did, it was about all the ways we've made this world easier for those who struggle. We reserved parking spots, built ramps, created closed captioning, dedicated elevators, and introduced special education. The world was a safe place where we could all live happily. Those with disabilities were just like everyone else—right?

Yet, as I walked with my son through life, it all became clear: The services we provide and the exceptions we make, those are all well and good, but they're not enough. The world is not a friendly or inviting place for those who are differently abled. There are more problems than solutions, and more ignorant people than kind ones. The world could be a cold, sad place, but it could also be bright, sunny, and filled with joy. It would take a heroic effort to find those safe, comfortable places for our boys, but I would never stop until we did.

Nineteen

M Y EYES ACHED AS I crept down the hallway toward Todd's office. It was 10 p.m. and I'd managed to get Conner, Cole, and Hunter down before feeding Dalton one last time. I'd switched him to formula to make sure he was gaining weight quickly so we could proceed with the implants. I loved his squishy legs and fluffy cheeks. Now, he was thriving and growing at an astonishing rate—healthy in every way but one.

I walked into Todd's office and approached him from behind as he sat in his chair in the warm glow of his computer screen, flipping through a stack of papers on his desk while simultaneously scrolling through a spreadsheet. I'd noticed in the past weeks that Todd had seemed distracted. We'd sit together at the end of the night to catch up on our favorite shows, and I'd glance at him only to notice him tapping on his phone. Sometimes I'd catch him staring into space; other times, he'd lose his train of thought mid-conversation. Something was just *off*.

I swallowed hard.

"What are you working on?" I asked.

"The budget," he said, his voice tight.

"Why are you doing that now? Let's just go to bed, we can do it in the morning."

"I can't go to bed now. I'm trying to figure out what we can do. All of this stuff with the banks, real estate, all of that—like you said, it's just... Lane, it's really bad."

Since the beginning of our marriage, I had managed our personal finances as well as those of Todd's business. I had alerted him a couple of weeks earlier of the housing market crisis, complete with inflated costs and bad loans. I took a deep breath and sighed.

"Everyone's having a hard time right now. It's not just us."

"I know, but so much of our money is tied up in real estate. I just can't see a way out of all this."

"I know things have been expensive with the boys, but it hasn't been that bad."

Todd dropped his head in his hands. I placed my hand on his back, wishing for something to say, but nothing came. Instead, I sank down next to him and put my hands on his knees.

"Are we going to lose the house?" I asked.

"We might," he managed.

His breath caught as his face blanched. I'd been so focused on the boys—the struggle with getting Conner and Cole into yet another new school, working on updating Conner's IEP as we began to experience new struggles, pushing to get Dalton onto every waiting list for implants, arranging appointments with counselors, setting up his IFSP, and doing everything that comes with the deaf diagnosis. It'd been so overwhelming that I hadn't made time to sit and talk to Todd about our finances in months. Now, we were dire straits. There, in the dim light of the office, I wiped tears from my cheeks, letting the truth overwhelm me: Things were bad, and they would likely get a whole lot worse.

For the next few years, our finances and business took over our lives in addition to juggling the unique needs of our four boys. Due to financial losses, our family was forced out of our beloved home, and we bounced from rental to rental, waiting for things to improve. It was a tumultuous time period that saw Dalton receiving his cochlear implants. After the surgery, Todd and I perched at the end of his hospital bed, staring at the familiar domes over his ears and his face squished beneath thick layers of bandages. We watched him heal, followed the IFSP, began taking him to Listen & Talk, ushered him into OT, and took all of the steps we'd learned to take through our work with Conner. The road was bumpy and rutted, paved with disappointments, struggles, and constant pressure to adjust our course as various systems and institutions continued to fail us.

Dalton went from a toddler to a preschool-aged little boy, all video games, comic books, toy cars, and cartoons. Sometimes I'd stare at him wrestling with his brothers and I'd lose my breath; somehow, in all the chaos, our youngest wasn't so young anymore. One Friday evening as I sat on our small, worn couch making my to-do list in our dingy rental, Todd sent me a text:

Let's get dinner tonight, just the two of us.

I pressed my lips together. My brain started flipping through all the things that had to get done that afternoon and evening: Dalton had OT, Hunter had tutoring, Conner had an eye doctor's appointment, and Cole had soccer practice. I had a list of emails to respond to from various therapists and specialists. All of the activities and appointments and to do items were tied in a giant knot in my brain, and no matter how badly I tried, I couldn't see a way to get free for an hour, let alone the time it would take to eat a full meal. I quickly replied:

"We have a busy night. I don't think we can make it work."

Todd fired back:

"There's never a good time. I'll get us a reservation."

I clenched my teeth, frustrated that Todd was pushing this. We were still watching our finances and trying to catch up from the losses we'd incurred. There was a constant accumulation of tasks to get done, and if one thing slipped, it would just get added to the agenda for the next day—and so on and so on. Our life was a constant snowball of things to do, people to talk to, and fires to put out. I wasn't sure how to tell Todd that a date night wasn't a priority right now, so I shook my head and responded:

"Ok."

Later that evening, I sat across from Todd in a dim restaurant, shifting in my chair as he perused the menu. I was painfully aware of the fact that my jeans still felt too tight nearly five years after giving birth to Dalton. My belly hung slightly over the waistband, my blouse was sitting wrong over my chest, and my unwashed hair felt greasy. All I could think about was the boys at home with the sitter—were they doing their homework? Did I remember to ask the sitter to switch the clothes from the washer to the dryer? If I didn't, the clothes might have that smell they got when they stayed in the machine for too long, and I'd have to run them again. With this thought, I scrambled for my phone in my purse and quickly tapped a message to the sitter as Todd closed his menu and poured more wine into my glass.

"Everything okay?" he asked.

"It's fine, I just forgot to mention something when we left the house." He reached across the table and gestured for me to place my hands in his. I forced a smile and reached out, letting his hands envelop mine.

"I feel like I haven't seen you at all this week," he said.

"Also, Conner's English teacher asked for a conference," I replied. "This is, like, the third time. I'm not sure what's going on with her. She honestly seems like she has it out for him. I keep checking his work and it's fine. Maybe I should call the principal—"

"Lane, can we try to put those things aside right now and just focus on us?"

My stomach dropped. I automatically yanked my hands back, my left arm grazing my water glass, which nearly toppled off the table. I wanted to scream at him, to tell him that there was no *us* outside of all this. We were in this together. The constant chaos, the busyness, the needs to meet, the storm of stuff to deal with—they were a part of the fabric of our family. To extract ourselves from it, even for a moment, felt frivolous. I just wanted him to understand. Sensing my frustration, Todd reached for my hands again.

"I just don't want everything we have going on to be *all* we have going on," he said.

"I know," I said, signaling for the waiter. "Let's just order our food."

Todd pulled his hand back and reopened his menu. As the waiter approached, I noticed the flickering light of the table's small candle highlighting Todd's wrinkled brow. I knew he was upset, but the truth was, he wanted more of me than I was able to give. In order to make our lives work, sacrifices had to be made.

No matter which way you cut it, when your life is a swirl of insanity, the easiest place to trim the fat and free up time is by pushing your own needs aside. I didn't need to exercise, shower every day, or read a book at night. I didn't need to spend time connecting with Todd. I didn't need to nurture any relationships at all. What I needed was more time to dedicate to the boys, my job. Those were the things that mattered. The rest could wait until sometime in the future when I was ready to start *living* again.

Twenty

I SAT STARING AT my computer screen in the stark, halogen light of my office, the cursor blinking on a blank page. I had so much work to do, but my mind was completely blank. My eyes were hot, lids heavy. I hadn't slept much, if at all, the night before. Since he was scared of the dark like Conner was, Dalton had had a restless night of sleep, causing me to leap from bed dozens of times. When I was finally able to close my eyes, dawn came too soon. Now, I was perched on my stiff, ergonomic chair, trying to make myself do something—anything. Exasperated, I pushed my chair back and shuffled to the coffee maker, filling my favorite mug to the brim.

Back at my computer, I decided I would finish my cup of coffee before I started my project, to get some caffeine in my system when I needed it most. I navigated my mouse to the search engine, typed in the surrounding area codes, and entered the words "house for sale." This was my favorite thing to do during down time: to scroll page after page after page, dreaming about putting down roots in a home that really felt *ours*. The downturn we'd survived was beginning to recede; I had been made full-time at my job, Todd's work was picking up steam, and we were returning money to the savings account that we'd all but drained. It finally seemed like a house was within reach.

I scrolled through pages of small ranch homes, duplexes, townhouses, and large fixer-uppers with a lot of "character." That's when my eyes landed on an older house by a lake that needed a lot of work. As soon as I saw the price, I clicked on the listing to enlarge the image. Once it loaded on my screen and as I clicked through images of the exterior, I began to perk up. The house was in our dream location, on a lake I'd always fantasized about living on. The square footage, the location (within walking distance to a highly rated elementary school), the landscaping, the views—it was all almost too perfect. I immediately dialed Todd, who answered after just one ring,

"Hey, what's going on?" he asked.

"Todd, I found the most perfect house. Are you by your computer?"

"A house? When did you have time to do that?"

"I was just taking a break for some coffee and scrolled a bit. I'm sending you the link now."

The line was quiet as I listened to Todd's fingers striking his keyboard. I flipped through the pictures again, my stomach doing acrobatics.

"Did you get it?" I asked. "Isn't it amazing? Look at the location!"

"Wow, okay. We need to see it so I can really assess it. I can't believe you found this—the price isn't bad, either."

"Right! We could come in low, too."

"Let me call the listing agent—I'll get us in for a showing tonight if I can."

I put the phone down and picked up my now-lukewarm cup of coffee. I didn't want to get too far ahead of myself, but something felt so right about this house. I could really picture myself there. I could see the boys playing in the yard, fishing off the dock, and running in the backyard. I imagined myself in the kitchen, sipping my morning coffee while looking out over the sparkling lake. It was perfectly imperfect, and I couldn't wait to see it for myself.

Later that evening, we stood at the water's edge as the sun made its way below the horizon. We'd toured the house, which despite a distinct mildewy smell was exactly as I'd imagined it. Todd and I moved from room to room, discussing the things we'd change, how the remodel would go, and where the boys would sleep. Then, we wandered out onto the lawn and locked eyes, smiling as we spoke through the particulars of a future we both so desperately wanted: A place of our own, somewhere that would finally feel like home after all we'd been through. The very next day, we put in an offer below asking. To our surprise, it was immediately accepted. Within the next month, we began moving out of our last rental, which had never felt like home anyway.

Conner sat on his bed reading as Dalton and Hunter did their homework at a corner table. I glanced out the window at the lake with a happy heart. It was nearing six months since we'd made the move, and it was one of the happiest times we'd had in years. We played games, watched movies, and cozied up together every night, sharing inside jokes and belly laughs. Sure, there were times when the boys fought, Todd and I argued, and the newness felt hard to navigate, but those moments passed quickly. I'd become adept at gazing out over the water and wandering through the house, reminding myself that we were headed toward something amazing. Even now as I pulled cans of soda out of the refrigerator, my stomach fizzled with joy.

"Dinner!" I called out.

Cole bounded down the stairs as Conner put down his book and Dalton and Hunter thundered to the table. Todd walked in just as I opened the pizza box and pulled out an extra cheesy piece for Dalton.

"Pizza night!" Todd said, pulling off his jacket and laying it on Hunter's nearby bed. "We're getting so close to being able to move in the house, guys! It's looking good for us to start moving our things in next week. How was everyone's day?"

"Great," Dalton squealed.

"It was okay," Cole responded. "Got my math test back. I got an A."

"Awesome, man, great job!" said Todd.

"Mine was good, but school was boring," Hunter said with a sigh.

"Sorry to hear that, buddy," I replied. "What about you, Conner?"

I looked across the table at Conner. While his brothers were jamming pizza in their mouths and sipping from their cans of soda, he remained stoic. I glanced at Todd, who had taken notice too.

"Conner, you okay?" he asked.

"I'm fine, Dad."

I looked at Cole who mouthed, "Bad day."

"Want to talk about anything?" I asked.

He shook his head and poked at his pizza.

With my throat a little tighter, I went back to eating. Conner had been quiet for days on end, busying himself with homework and then a book or video game after school. He wasn't his normal chatty self, but I assumed he was just adjusting to the new house—we just had to push through the awkward moving phase. But Cole's words gave me pause. This wasn't just an environmental thing; it was something more.

After we got settled into the new house, I came home after a long, stressful day at the office. I'd had back-to-back meetings, which meant that I didn't get any of my regular work done and spent the day feeling completely behind. Once I hung up my jacket, I immediately started pulling out snacks for the boys—they were always ravenous when they got home. I heard the deep rumble of the bus and the squeal of the brakes. Moments later, Cole walked into the kitchen and reached for a bowl of fruit before saying, "Hi, Mom."

"Where's Conner?" I asked.

Just then, Conner shuffled into the kitchen and dropped his bag on the floor, then slid into a chair at the kitchen table. I walked over to him and pulled out a seat. His glasses were smudged and his cheeks were red. He'd been crying.

"Conner, what's wrong?" I asked.

"Nothing," he replied.

"It's *not* nothing," Cole interjected.

Conner shot him a look.

"What? It's not," he replied.

"What is it?" I asked.

"If you're not going to say it, I am," Cole said to Conner.

Conner stayed quiet, averting his puffy eyes.

"Fine," Cole replied. "Conner is being ignored and totally left out by the kids in his class. I've been trying to help, but they don't want to hang out with him. We told the principal, but—"

"And the principal hasn't done anything?" I asked.

"No," Conner said, rubbing his eyes. "It's worse every day. They never let me sit with them, they never choose me for group projects, they... they don't like me."

"I'll make a call right now," I promised. "Let me at least make them aware."

"There's no point in talking to the school, Mom. They won't do anything. And even if they do, it'll just make the kids hate me," Conner replied, slumping back in his chair.

"You've got to trust me. I'll figure this out."

He nodded.

"Conner, you have to tell me these things," I begged. "I can't help you if I don't know what's happening."

"I'm going to my room," he said, standing.

"Okay, but promise me."

"I promise," he said, grabbing his bag and walking out of the room.

I looked over at Cole, who was peeling pieces off a cheese stick.

"How bad is it?" I asked.

"It's really bad, Mom. He sits alone at lunch, and no one ever wants him as their partner. He's the first to get voted out when there's an uneven number of people for a game, and most kids just act like he doesn't exist. I mean, he dropped his books in the hallway today and people just stepped around him like he wasn't even there until I did something about it. I keep trying to ask them to be nicer to him, but nothing works." "But it's not your responsibility to fix this," I replied. "The school needs to handle this. I can't believe they're not doing anything."

"Someone just usually tells them to include him. They do, but then they start ignoring him again as soon as no one's watching."

"Thanks for telling me. And thanks for always watching out for him. He's lucky to have you," I said, giving him a side hug.

"He's my brother," he said, shrugging.

After Cole left the room, I sat at the table and took a deep breath as I reached for my phone. I felt physically sick. When you have a child with disabilities, no one ever prepares you for the isolation they'll face. Kids can be mean spirited, hurtful, and cruel. As parents, we're forced to walk a fine line between giving them life experience among kids who don't share the same challenges and keeping them safe amongst their differently-abled peers. Although an inclusive approach is best, it's impossible to know how to handle the ignorance they face. It requires an excellent, dedicated team who keep their eyes on the child, keeping them safe and keeping the parents informed.

Without fail, whenever we started at a new school, I sat down with the principal and the rest of his team to go over Conner's IEP. Those meetings were always filled with smiles and sympathetic nods. The teams seem cohesive, strong, and motivated to help him succeed. Yet, every time—and I mean every single time—the wheels fell off as soon as the school year got underway. Those same teachers and administrators would lose steam and stop caring, and a child who once seemed like the most important person in the world to them would suddenly seem like a burden. I couldn't see a solution. I felt constantly crushed beneath a truth that was slowly revealing itself to me: There *was* no solution. It was all just luck of the draw.

Dreading my upcoming conversation with the principal, I punched the number for the school into my phone and placed it to my ear. Each ring slashed through me until the receptionist picked up.

"Mr. Banks' office?"

"Hi, this is Lane McKittrick, Conner McKittrick's mom. We've had some incidents that I need to discuss with Mr. Banks. Can I speak with him, please?"

There was silence on the end of the phone, then the rustling of papers. Finally, she responded, "I'm sorry, he'll have to call you back."

"Please tell him it's urgent," I replied, then hung up the phone.

I stood in the hallway at the small neighborhood elementary school that Hunter and Dalton attended. The boys had been there for several months, and were loving everything about the school. The short drive there, down tree-lined streets and sidewalks crowded with kids running and roughhousing on the way to school, was beautiful. Thus far, things had seemed okay with Dalton, but Hunter had recently begun to show signs of trouble. He'd come home frustrated, crying about his teacher and whining that he couldn't do anything right. After several unanswered calls and emails to his teacher, I made an appointment for an in-person meeting to discuss what was going on with Hunter, because something just wasn't right. Now, I stood in the hallway staring at scribbled drawings and painted pictures taped to the brick walls. My eyes danced down the rows until I found something of Hunter's—a half-painted picture of a pumpkin. I stooped to look at it just as the teacher's shoes clicked toward me and stopped at the classroom door.

"Mrs. McKittrick?" she asked.

"Hi, Mrs. Cooper—please, call me Lane. It's good to see you," I said, following her into the classroom.

"I'm sorry we've been missing one another, but I'm so glad you're here now—please take a seat," she said, motioning to a child-sized chair in front of her desk, which I squeezed myself into.

"Thanks for making the time to see me," I said. "I've been wanting to speak to you about Hunter. He seems frustrated, like he's having a hard time. Can you help me understand what's going on?"

"Let me start by saying that Hunter is a good kid," she said, leaning forward. "But to be honest, we've been having big issues with focus, concentration, and sometimes respect. He acts up in class frequently. I have trouble getting him to listen, which is essential if we want him to learn."

"Okay, can you give me a couple of examples?"

"Yes, I can offer a few. Just yesterday, we were painting pictures of pumpkins—"

"Yes, I just saw it outside," I said, gesturing. "It seemed like he didn't get to finish."

"That's because instead of painting like everyone else, he began jumping around and making faces, dancing, and trying to get his classmates to laugh," she explained sternly. "I asked him to stop several times, and he ignored me, so we had to take the paint away."

I wanted to scream: *He's SIX!* But I nodded instead.

"Also, he's having big issues with gripping his pencil. We've been training them to hold a pencil properly, and he cannot seem to get a handle on it. We've tried dozens of them and we've even sent a few home. Have you seen them in his bag?"

"Yes—we've worked with him too, and we know that's an issue, but he seems to be improving."

"In class, he gets *extremely* upset when we correct him. It's something that's becoming very, very disruptive." I gritted my teeth. Here we were, in the same place with Hunter that I'd so often found myself with Conner and Dalton. Teachers were willing to point out all of the problems, but they wouldn't offer any solutions.

"Okay," I responded. "Should we speak with a special ed teacher?"

"Well, that's not something I can do for you. I'll give you her contact information."

I stared at Mrs. Cooper, who had a placating smile on her face, and wanted to tell her that she was bad at her job. Instead, I pulled both Dalton and Hunter right then.

Todd and I quickly put them back into private school for a more nurturing environment, but that choice meant sacrificing some of the services that public schools provide. At the new school, we had a care team that included a teacher of the blind and low vision, but there was no teacher of the deaf, nor was there a special education teacher on the team. This placed even more of the onus on Todd and me to bring resources to the table. I was, therefore, desperately trying to lead teams for all three of my boys, finding ways to help them get the best education with respect to their unique needs. All of my energy went to carefully curating their care as best I could with teams that never failed to underperform, and I was overworked and exhausted.

I knew that my first step needed to be an evaluation for Hunter—maybe he was dealing with learning disabilities or sensory processing issues, or maybe he was acting out because of all that comes with having disabled family members. The only way to know was to put in the work, and I'd have to do it alone—just like everything else.

We were able to get a tutor assigned to Hunter and slowly saw him make incremental improvements with my constant help, but staying on the school became another full-time job. I found myself disappearing under the crushing pressure. Between Conner's school struggles, Hunter's behavioral issues, and Dalton's special needs, there was hardly a moment for me to breathe, let alone put an ounce of care into myself or anyone else. My relationship with Todd had become distant, strained, and transactional. We were business partners. We tag-teamed the boys' care as much as possible, but other than that, we were in our own separate worlds.

Although Dalton's hearing loss and eyesight had remained the same, he had to adjust to an increased workload in school. Of course, as time went on, his classes became more challenging, work got harder, and grading was more intense. Soon, Dalton became hysterical anytime he had to go to school, which was becoming a massive problem. I was so strictly scheduled that I didn't have a minute of extra time between school drop-off and heading to work. The tiniest delay would make me late, which meant that I was spending mornings overwhelmed by tantrums, sweating and anxious as I tried to coax Dalton out of the car gently but firmly. Once I was finally able to get him through the door of the school, he would hang on my legs and have to be pulled off so I could rush out while choking back tears. I was often overwhelmed by sadness and anger when I arrived at my office, mentally rearranging my calendar to make up for the lost time. I spent my entire life late for everything, in a constant state of panic that I wasn't keeping up.

As Christmas break neared and I found myself dragging Dalton across an icy, salt-dusted parking lot, I decided it was time to take action. This wasn't just anxiety or a small behavioral quirk. Something else was going on—and the longer things went on, the more severe

Dalton's issues became. He would freeze at the thought of work on the horizon—any work at all. A school project one month out would become a crushing point of contention. He couldn't sleep, had trouble eating, and couldn't bring himself to take any steps toward a solution. I spent countless hours trying to talk him off the ledge about the smallest things, but it was often time wasted. Once he was over the edge, it was nearly impossible to bring him back.

I'd been in touch with the school and pulled as much information as I could from Hunter about what was going on, but he didn't seem to know anything either. The only insight teachers could give was that he tended to be a perfectionist. He liked to get things right, and he wanted to please everyone. When teachers would come around to ask if he was okay, he'd smile and say, "Yes!" He always seemed happy and eager to complete his work; he gave them no cause for concern. Yet, none of this matched what we were seeing at home. Something wasn't adding up.

I started scrupulously observing everything Dalton did when it came to school. His behavior wasn't like Hunter's; he wasn't all over the place, running around and tough to corral. At first, I thought it was just fatigue, which is common with kids who have combined hearing and vision loss. but that didn't seem to fit. When the thought occurred to me that it seemed like he was having a trauma response to his homework, I considered that Dalton might actually be struggling in a similar way to Hunter—maybe his symptoms were just presenting themselves differently.

Soon, we found ourselves back in the office where we'd had Hunter evaluated for ADHD. I sat in the stuffy room in a hard plastic chair next to Dalton, listening as he answered each of the evaluator's questions.

"Is it hard for you to wake up in the morning?" the doctor asked.

"I don't like waking up," Dalton mumbled, swinging his legs.

"Is it hard for you to get ready quickly?"

"Yeah."

"Do you find yourself getting distracted?"

He glanced at me and nodded.

"Yeah, usually," he said.

My eyes drifted to a poster on the wall with a mountain on it with the phrase *You can move mountains!* scrawled across it. I knew we were speeding toward the inevitable: yet another diagnosis for my sweet son. The evaluator adjusted his glasses.

"Dalton, we're all done here," he said. "Why don't you head out into the waiting room and check out some of the books we have out there?"

Dalton stood and swiped his jacket off the chair before leaving the room.

"He's got ADHD, doesn't he?" I asked, scooting forward in the plastic chair.

"It seems so," the evaluator replied, jogging the stack of papers he was holding. "The thing is, he also seems to be dealing with anxiety—some really severe anxiety. I would suggest talking to a psychiatrist. My guess is that the combination of ADHD, anxiety, and all that comes with Usher syndrome is causing him big issues in school. It's a lot for a kid to handle. I think it'd be best for you to take a look at his IEP again."

I wanted to cry. I knew the IEP needed work, and I knew I had to gather his team, but I also knew what lay ahead. Trying to finesse an IEP could be maddening, and no matter how hard I tried, the reality was that I did not have the knowledge or understanding to perfect the boys' IEPs to make them work. I'd been trying with Conner for all of his schooling, and he was a teenager now.

At the precipice of these new adjustments, I felt determined but sad. I, too, had anxiety. I knew what Dalton must've been dealing with, but there wasn't an easy fix. Resources at the school were limited; the teachers were nice but busy. Dalton's own teacher was in line to become a principal, so she was in and out a lot, causing Dalton to have substitutes several times per week. It meant that every day was filled with the unknown. He never knew what he was going to get when he walked through the doors of the school, so it was no wonder he spent so much time on the verge of hysteria.

The evaluator slid several pamphlets across the table.

"These are for you," he said. "I know I gave you some for Hunter, but this one is about anxiety."

He tapped his finger on a brochure with a group of smiling kids on the front—all apparently thrilled about their journeys with anxiety. I wondered what it would be like if the pamphlets featured realistic images: pictures of sad, tired eyes, of parents overcome by grief, of half-finished homework and tests with bad grades scribbled at the top.

I took the pamphlet and tucked it into my purse before heading back into the cold Seattle air, clutching Dalton's little hand in mine as if he might accidentally fly away.

Twenty-One

SOMETIMES A THOUGHT COMES to you that takes hold in an instant—something so obvious that your mind can't help but grasp it as truth. It hits you like a bolt of lightning, bursting through your body like a jolt of indescribable energy. It moves you in ways that nothing ever has.

It happened on a rare quiet evening in the house. I'd poured myself a glass of wine and headed out to the back porch to stare out over the lake. As my eyes fell on a fat star twinkling above, I began to think about the gaps in my knowledge. If I were to wish for anything on that star, I'd wish for a special ed teacher dedicated to our family, someone who would stick with us all the way through the boys' schooling and beyond.

That's when it dawned on me: I could *be* that person.

I could get my PhD in Special Education.

Oh my gosh.

It had been *me* all along.

I suddenly realized that if I wanted the best out of a team, I had to be the best member of the team—and I could only do that if I had the knowledge and understanding that special education teachers brought to the table. With ever-evolving teams at school, constantly shifting staff dynamics, and constant ups and downs, there had to be someone reliable at the helm. That someone was always me, but it hadn't dawned on me that I could be even more effective with one more thing under my belt: education.

But as soon as I had that thought, I pushed the entire idea aside. There was no way. The timing—it was just awful. The next morning, juggling a notebook and a cup of coffee, I knocked softly on my boss Sandra's office door.

"Hey, come in!" she said with a smile. "Let me just finish this one email and we can start."

I stepped over the threshold and closed the door behind me with a *click* before sitting and placing my notebook on her desk. Sandra's long, natural nails tapped at the keyboard, her lips pressed together as she typed. As much as I loved Sandra, who had been my boss for many years, I couldn't quell my nerves. She was about to give me my annual review. Although I knew I'd done great work, I couldn't ignore the fact that I was often late, sometimes distracted, and had been so overcome with emotion on so many days that my productivity had suffered. On the inside, I felt like a mess, but it was hard to gauge how it was being perceived.

"Okay, sending now," she said, narrowing her eyes. "There—done!" She adjusted her chair to face mine before opening a folder and pulling a pen from a nearby cup. "First things first: How are the boys?"

"They're doing well," I replied. "Lots going on, as usual."

"And you? How are you feeling?"

"Good," I said, folding my hands in my lap. "A little nervous."

"About the review? Lane, please. You have nothing to worry about."

I knitted my eyebrows together.

"Look, it's no secret that you've been going through a lot," Sandra said. "I know how hard you work for your boys. I imagine you really have no downtime at all. I see all that, I do—but despite all of it, your work here has been excellent."

"Thank you, I just—" I began. To my horror, my eyes were beginning to tear up.

"Lane, listen," Sandra gently interrupted. "I know what you're thinking. The challenges you face outside of here likely make you feel like you're spread too thin. That may be true, but you really are keeping up here. Your work continues to be solid. You're quick to make arrangements if anything is delayed, you stay on top of your inbox even when I know you're juggling appointments." She set her pen down and waited to catch my eye. "You're doing a great job."

My shoulders dropped. I drew a breath to compose myself.

"I really appreciate you saying that," I said. "Things have just been so crazy for so long that it's easy to feel like I'm not doing anything right."

"But you are! I'd argue that you're doing nearly *everything* right. You're a human being."

I nodded, blinking the tears away.

"Lane, I have to ask: What do you see in your future here at University of Washington?"

"I love working here. You've been so amazing with me, and I can't thank you enough. I guess right now I'm just looking into the future at my next promotion."

"Right," Sandra replied, leaning forward. "And do you feel excited about it? This next promotion will mean more work on the financial side. Does that excite you?"

I picked at my thumbnail, trying to formulate a response. I'd spent all of my life working in roles that were focused on sales, driven by dollar signs more than anything else. As much as money had always driven me, the work was beginning to feel... empty. I shrugged my shoulders.

"Honestly, I don't know," I replied finally.

"Okay," she said with a nod. "And what do you want to do in the future? When you really think about it honestly, what do you want to be known for?"

I'd never allowed myself to think about it that way before; I'd been so focused on supporting the family, financially and otherwise, that I hadn't thought about my own goals beyond providing the best possible life for everyone around me. And that was the thing—the crux of it all. The truth was, what I'd uncovered the night before had revealed a stark truth about my life: Advocating for the boys had become more than a thing I *had* to do. It had become my passion. Learning about special education wouldn't just be an exercise in learning to better help the boys—it would open doors for me to improve the landscape for children with special needs on a much larger scale.

"I think I want to pursue a career in special education," I said.

"Lane, that's *amazing*," Sandra replied. "I completely understand that, and I think it's perfect for you."

I kept my lips pursed and nodded.

"Please, though—don't go anywhere quite yet. Take your time, explore your options, and continue to work with me. We'll handle everything as it comes."

Sandra and I sat and talked, sipping coffee for over an hour. She helped me brainstorm, gave me ideas, and even had thoughts on schools I could contact. By the time I pushed my chair back and stood, I was breathless, full of both excitement and fear and terrified that saying everything out loud made it true. The next step was to speak to Todd, the thought of which made my stomach churn. It would be a big adjustment for him, but he had to understand. I hoped he could find it in his heart to be supportive.

That evening, I said goodnight to the boys one by one and made my way downstairs to the living room where Todd sat in a beam of lamplight, scrolling on his phone. I turned off the kitchen light and walked toward the couch, where I took a seat next to him. I waited for him to notice me, then chuckled when it became clear he was too focused on his phone to hear me enter the room.

"Was your day all right?" I asked.

"It was fine," he replied, still looking at his phone. "You?"

"It was good, yeah" I said, nodding. "So—I had my review with Sandra today."

"Oh, yeah? How was it?" he asked.

"It was good. We talked about a lot of stuff. About my future with the school."

"Your future, huh?" he asked, looking up.

"Yeah, I mean—Sandra pushed me to think about my long-term goals. I guess it scared me to think about it a little."

Todd put his phone down on the coffee table and turned to face me.

"What do you mean?" he asked. I dried my palms on my gray pajama pants and steeled myself.

"Todd, I think I want to leave my job and focus on special education for real. Not just for the boys," I said, gesturing to their rooms, "but in a professional capacity."

"Wait," he said, narrowing his eyes. "*Leave* your job?"

"Well," I hesitated, "not right away. I'll take my time in figuring out the next steps. I have to get into school, which will be a challenge in itself."

"Okay. I guess we'll figure it out."

He was trying to be supportive, but I could read between the lines. He wasn't thrilled with the idea and how it would impact the entire family. I knew it would push us further apart, but I was already numb, and I didn't care. I had to do something for myself for once.

"Can we talk about this more?" I asked. "I'd really like to know what you think."

"How are you going to add one more thing onto your plate?" he asked.

"And what will that mean for our relationship?" He paused to steady himself. "I'll support you, of course I will. I always do."

I nodded. I knew Todd was trying to be supportive, even though he wasn't happy that I would be stretched even thinner.

"I hope it'll be good for all of us in the end. It'll take work, but—I need to do this," I said quietly, slumping back on the couch. I stared out the window, despondent. The moon was bright and full, casting a twinkling ray of light onto the black water below. I thought back to the beginning with Todd—the way we moved in sync, the way we'd once loved one another, the way his love always felt like home to me. I always thought we'd weather every storm together, but now things felt different. Just as I began to feel the emotional toll of the difficult conversation, Todd returned to the room. He sat down next to me and put his hand on my knee, sighing deeply. I wanted to pull away, but I stayed still.

"Look, I'm sorry," he said softly. "I shouldn't have reacted like that. It's just a lot to take in. I support you. We'll figure it out."

I had nothing to say, so I nodded. He kissed me on the cheek and walked out of the room.

Imposter syndrome is real—I mean, *really* real—and it threatened to take me down as soon as I started looking into schools to attend. I knew from my research that most people pursuing PhDs in special education were already teachers who had years of experience under their belts. Who did I think I was stepping into this world?

Somehow, and after researching dozens of schools, I managed to push past the fear and anxiety and found myself in a phone interview with a faculty member from the University of Northern Colorado who specialized in deafblindness. I listened as she spoke about the school and the merits of their special education program.

"How does that all sound to you?" she asked finally.

"It sounds great. It would be a dream, honestly," I replied.

"So, Lane, tell me more about you. I see from your email that two of your children experience Usher syndrome. I'd imagine that's difficult and surely a big motivator for you."

"It is. And I know I don't have the educational background that I'm sure most of your applicants have, but I have a lot of experience."

She paused, perhaps checking a document in front of her.

"So, what would you say is the greatest problem with education today?" she asked.

I froze; my mind went completely blank. I knew there were problems, but I didn't know how to define them on the spot. With my mouth dry, I tried to respond.

"Well, with my boys, the hardest thing has been building teams that are dedicated," I said. "My children often feel forgotten, as if giving them a passing grade and just moving them along to the next teacher is the easiest thing the school can do. I've spent so much time working on ways to help them get the education they deserve, but it's a fight."

She hummed in agreement.

"Sadly, your experience is the norm," she said. "It's why jobs in special education are so vital."

My nerves receded as she continued to ask me questions, nodding and smiling as I answered each one. By the time the interview was over, I was exhausted. She'd sounded excited at the end of the call and told me I'd be hearing from them soon, but I hung up with butterflies in my stomach. I so badly wanted to get in, but I knew I had no control over what their decision would be.

A few weeks later, Todd and I happened to be in Colorado on vacation. I hadn't yet heard whether I had been accepted to the PhD program, and I couldn't think of anything else. Impatient, I decided to risk an email to my interviewer—to see if we could meet in person and to put a face to a name. When she said yes, I was elated.

The very next day, Todd and I headed to campus, hand-in-hand. We strolled the tree-lined streets, gazing up at the snow-capped mountains beyond the pines.

"Good luck in there," he said with a smile.

"I'll see you soon," I replied.

What I hadn't expected was to leave the building with an acceptance letter in-hand! I felt like I was floating on cloud nine, and spent the next month getting ready to begin classes during the summer semester. I bought notebooks and pens, highlighters and post-its, and even a new bag to put all my stuff in. All were essential, if you asked me, even for virtual school. By the time I received my last textbook in the mail, I was ready to hit the ground running. Though most of my program was online, the first class was in-person in Colorado, and I couldn't wait.

On my first day of class, I swiped mascara on my lashes and dusted my cheeks with blush—rare for me at that time—before leaving my hotel to head to campus. I tried to steady my nerves as I looked around at my classmates. Everyone looked so studious—so young and so fresh.

Soon, the professor entered the room. She had a lot of energy as well as big, kind eyes, rosy cheeks, and short, red hair. She slid on a pair of red glasses and checked her watch. Just as the clock on my computer struck noon, she began to speak.

"Welcome everyone, I'm Professor Cullen," she said. "I am so thrilled that you have all made the choice to enter this field. We are in need of strong, dedicated, compassionate individuals like yourselves. Let's go around now and introduce ourselves. Let's start with you—Robin?"

One by one, my classmates piped up, stating their names, hobbies, and educational backgrounds. My stomach knotted as everyone listed their degrees, classroom work, and vast experience. By the time it was my turn, I could barely speak. I cleared my throat.

"Hi, I'm Lane McKittrick," I said. "I don't have a background like all of you. I'm just—I'm just a mom of kids with special needs."

"Hold on," Professor Cullen said, lifting her hand. "Did you say you're *just* a mom?"

"I did," I replied with a nod.

"Lane, is it?"

I nodded again.

"Lane, as a mother of children with special needs, you are more of an expert than any of us here. Yes, education is important, but you have lived experience, and that is beyond what any classroom can give you. I never want to hear you say that you are *just* anything again, okay?"

"Okay," I replied, my heart rate slowing. "Thank you."

She nodded.

"Very good," she said.

I looked around at my classmates. They were also nodding, and I felt something I had never felt before: validation. Overcome with emotion, I willed myself not to cry. I was finally in a place where the experiences I'd had with my boys were seen as my greatest strength—this despite the fact that I'd spent much of my life worrying that others would see my dedication to them as a weakness. I couldn't believe I had finally found a place where I was *seen*.

Twenty-Two

OVER THE NEXT FEW months, and with Todd and the boys' support, I began rigorously working my way through my PhD program. With no time for anything other than work and managing the boys' schedules, I had to squeeze my schooling into my lunch breaks and cram it into long nights and early mornings. The more I studied, the better I came to understand each and every one of the processes Todd and I had journeyed through with the boys. I was learning the language and discovering tiny nuances. I kept my work collaborative and quickly found ways to apply what I was learning to the boys' IEPs.

I was particularly focused on Dalton, whose team had finally come together. Now that I knew the landscape better than I did when Conner was his age, I was able to call the shots. Somehow, I was even finding time to volunteer with the PTA. Using every morsel of my time to make myself known to the school, I hosted events and planned bake sales. I also spent time in classrooms as a substitute teacher, earning college credit for the time I put in. Sometimes, despite the relationships I was building, my requests for changes to Dalton's education were met with blank stares or eye rolls, but I didn't care. I was learning how to best care for my son, and I was going to find ways to improve the team's ability to do so, too.

I was nearly two years into the program when I rushed into Dalton and Hunter's school for an afternoon of volunteering; I'd taken an afternoon off work to help with a group activity in Dalton's class. Running fifteen minutes behind (as usual), I darted into the office to sign in. As I scribbled my signature into the binder on the counter, the superintendent, Mr. Hagan stuck his head through his door.

"Mrs. McKittrick, can I see you before you leave?" he asked. "I just have something to go over with you."

"Sure," I replied with a nod.

I spent the next two hours darting from desk to desk in Dalton's classroom, helping the kids with group activities and eventually grabbing a stack of papers to grade for the teacher. When I finished the last one, I placed them neatly on the teacher's desk, said goodbye to Dalton, and strolled down the hallway. I headed into the office and stopped in front of the door to the principal's office, knocking on the wood next to the plaque with his name scrawled across it.

"Come in," Mr. Hagan said with a smile, light bouncing off his slick-looking bald head.

I smiled back and made my way inside. The office overlooked the parking lot, where buses were beginning to arrive. I set my bag on the floor and sighed.

"It's nice to sit down after all that," I said. "How are you doing?"

"Oh, I'm fine, thank you," he replied. "I want to tell you how much we appreciate all of the volunteer work you do around here—truly, it's incredible. How do you find the time?"

I laughed.

"Well, I don't have a life."

"I understand," he chuckled. "In that case, I have some filing I need help with."

"I'm on it!" I joked.

"Mrs. McKittrick," he continued, his smile fading. "In all seriousness, I wanted to sit down with you today to offer you a little perspective on some... challenges we're having."

"Okay," I responded, tilting my head.

"As you know, we've worked hard at the school to put together a comprehensive team to help the boys—Dalton in particular. We've brought in a student support specialist, Mrs. Green, and she's very knowledgeable about special education."

"Right, and I've been so appreciative of that."

"And you're a big part of that team. However, unfortunately, Mrs. McKittrick, we at the school feel as though you might be *too* big a part of the team."

I swallowed hard.

"I worry that your involvement is beginning to be the opposite of helpful," he continued. "We find ourselves in a situation now where the team members find it difficult to do their jobs because of the way you've inserted yourself."

Blood rushed to my face—molten hot.

"Let me stop you right there," I said, wringing my hands in my lap. "I'm not just a mom trying to worm her way in. I'm working on my PhD in special education. I know what I'm doing, and when I request changes, there's a reason. I bring expertise in deafblindness—an expertise that no one else has."

"That may be so, but it's frequent—and frankly, it's disruptive. The team feels that you're overstepping, and I tend to agree. You need to leave it to us: the professionals."

I tried to catch my breath as Mr. Hagan went on about the drawbacks of my involvement and all the ways I was ruining Dalton's schooling by "inserting myself." My entire life as a mom had been dedicated to riding the wave of these ineffective teams, fighting for adequate care and striving to make things better. Now, I'd finally done it. I'd finally gotten us all to a place where we felt good—*better* than good. We felt amazing. Now, I was sitting across from a sad, old man set on dismantling everything I'd worked so hard to build.

"I'm done with this," I announced, shoving my chair back. "What you're saying goes against all the research on this subject. Parents are important members of their children's education teams, and their views are important. They should be included in *every* aspect!"

"Mrs. McKittrick, I'm sorry you're upset."

"I'm not upset, I'm *angry*. I have dedicated every spare second to this school, and this is how you choose to treat me? Dalton is thriving—*finally!*"

"That may be, but we think it would be more efficient if you just let us do our job."

I was so full of rage that I didn't dare speak another word. I clumsily gathered up my bag, in my arms and rushed out of the office, not bothering to say goodbye to the receptionist. I rushed to my car, yanked the door open, and nearly threw my body into the driver's seat before bursting into tears.

I'd worked so hard and put so much into the process of learning exactly what to do to get the best education for the boys, and I had gotten us exactly nowhere. The grief felt crushing. I was suddenly thrust into a situation where I needed to rethink everything I'd done, recap every conversation I'd had, and take drastic action. I pulled out my phone as the school's pick-up line began to build. I tapped at the screen trying to figure out who to call, but my mind was blank. I couldn't call my mom; she didn't understand the nuances of our struggles. And my friends? No one truly understood. I was quickly realizing that I didn't have a single friend I could call in a crisis, leaving me isolated as my world crumbled around me.

Eventually, I called Todd. I could barely breathe. I knew he was busy at work and hadn't been involved enough to understand the gravity of what had happened but he understood all the energy I put into making school the best for our kids. Todd was instantly upset and ready to march down to the school to give Mr. Hagan a piece of his mind for treating me so poorly. Even though Todd and I sometimes struggled, he was showing up for me now. He was all I had, despite the fact that our relationship wasn't perfect.

I managed to get myself home, where I paced around the house. I rubbed my chest, trying to return to a calm, logical state, but my breaths became shallower and sped up until I was fighting off an anxiety attack. *Just make a plan,* I willed myself. I knew I couldn't allow the kids to stay at that school. It wasn't the incredible place I thought it was—there were big, cavernous cracks in the foundation, and I couldn't let that smug superintendent get the best of me. In the meantime, I'd stop doing every bit of volunteering. They didn't deserve my time.

I poured myself an ill-advised cup of late afternoon coffee and headed to my computer, set on researching schools. We'd switched so many times I'd lost count, but I was still determined to find somewhere I could send the boys that would support the type of collaborative care I'd learned was best for special needs children. As I wiggled the mouse to wake my computer, my email happened to be open, and I saw a mass email from Mr. Hagan. The subject line was "Principal for a Day."

I felt sick. Principal for a Day was an event that the whole school looked forward to. It was a privilege raffled off by the PTA, and the winner got to do the morning announcements, shadow the principal, and spend a whole day feeling like the school's fearless leader. Todd and I had outbid everyone to give Dalton the chance to get to spend the day with Mr. Hagan. When he'd won, it was as if he'd won the lottery—he loved every single second of it. He'd acted as Principal for a Day that past Thursday and came home glowing, excitedly giving us all the details.

Now, staring at candid photos of Mr. Hagan and Dalton spending a whole day together, it made me nauseous to see Dalton beaming at the camera next to the man who single-handedly decided to destroy all we'd worked so hard for. I felt like a caged animal. I was perpetually trapped in a world where no one consistently cared about the boys' well-being. I couldn't do another round of fake smiles, feigned enthusiasm, and empty encouragement. Something had to change—something big.

Once again, we were in transition. Hunter and Dalton were starting at new schools, which meant all four of our kids would be getting educated separately. This time, I approached the school staff confident in the education I was receiving, presenting myself as a qualified team member in my children's care from the start. Dalton's IEP had been adjusted, and his team was working with him on new goals. Hunter was in middle school, and he was getting the support he needed; the entire curriculum was online, making it so much more accessible for him. Cole was excelling academically and involved in athletics, and Conner was speeding toward graduation. I couldn't believe how far we'd come on our journey as a family.

In my PhD program, I was starting to make strides toward a specialization I didn't even know existed. I'd taken an IEP law class, something that seemed so foreign to me despite the years I'd been working on these plans with my children and their care teams. Suddenly, it all began to make sense to me: The IEP system wasn't cut and dry—there were tons of tiny nuances, loopholes, and areas of opportunity.

With Conner at the precipice of graduation, it was time for the annual review of his IEP. I was proactive and requested a copy before the meeting so I could review it. I scrolled through page after page, stopping on a list of non-specific goals that the team had somehow proposed: submitting homework on time, never being late for class. I realized that this was what happened at most transition IEP meetings when students were present but not actively involved. Teams weren't engaging the children; instead, they were making goals for them without much forethought and, many times, parents didn't want them there because the meetings were so deficit-based. This often left children with IEPs that weren't actually designed to give them the futures they desired. It seemed like his team's only goal was to fill in the form's blanks with *something*.

I printed the IEP, pushed my chair back from my desk, and made my way to Conner's room. I knocked on the door frame and waved.

"Can I come in?" I asked.

"Sure, what's up?" he replied, pushing his homework aside.

"We have your IEP meeting tomorrow afternoon, and I want to go over a few things with you before we go in. Is that okay?"

He nodded.

I crossed the room and sat on his bed, shoving a pile of books aside. I glanced around at game consoles, clothes, and a small pile of shoes in the corner. It struck me that his room was no longer filled with toys—no Legos to step on and no action figures to kick aside. It was showing all the signs of maturity. Conner was growing up, which was all the more reason to tackle his IEP now, before it was too late. I turned to face him.

"All right, do you remember reviewing this with your team last year?" I asked.

"I guess so," he replied.

"Well, here it lists your goals. It talks about turning your homework in on time and working on braille. Do you have more specific goals in mind?"

"I mean, I don't know what those goals have to do with my future," he said with a shrug.

"Okay, well now is the time to talk about that stuff, buddy. What do you think about all this? How do you see your life playing out after high school?"

As I sat on Conner's navy-blue bedspread, I had my first honest conversation with my son about his IEP. To an outsider, this might seem like something miniscule, but for Conner and me, it was revolutionary. For the first time ever, I was able to look at the IEP as something collaborative that I could work on with Conner rather than allowing a team to do it for us. This time, heading into the meeting, I was prepared to do more than just sit and listen. And Conner felt the same way.

The next day, Conner and I sat side-by-side in the school counselor's office, which was crowded with Dalton's counselor, special ed teacher, teacher of the deaf, teacher of the blind, and the principal. Once we all greeted one another, the counselor went around the circle and handed out collated copies of Conner's IEP.

"Okay, everyone," the counselor said, "let's take a few moments to read this over, and then we can each share our thoughts."

"Sir, let me interrupt for a moment," I said, raising my hand. "Conner and I took some time to review this last night, and he has some thoughts—especially regarding the goal section. Some of these lines are blank, and some of them have goals on them, but they aren't specific, nor do they pertain to what Conner actually wants for his future."

The teacher of the blind and low vision visibly stiffened.

"I understand," he replied. "We look forward to hearing your thoughts."

"The thing is though, Conner is here—I'd like to let him speak to all this. Go ahead, buddy," I urged.

Conner cleared his throat.

"Yes, I looked over the document with my mom last night," he began. "All of the goals set are things I already do—like handing in my homework on time. I know that I want to go to college, but I don't know exactly where. I want to get a degree in social sciences or some related field, and I want to move into the dorms like everyone else."

I beamed as I listened to Conner keep sharing his future goals. His voice was confident, and his stance was steady. I found myself wondering when this had all happened. Somewhere along the way, my little boy had become a man.

As Conner and I continued to collaborate with the team, we began to uncover new goals we hadn't ever thought of. Thus far, we'd been so focused on academics that we hadn't yet begun to educate Conner on independent living. We now had a host of goals, from teaching Conner to do his own laundry to showing him how to do some simple cooking. We also created goals regarding assistive technology and discovering every available way to make his life easier.

Before we knew it, we'd built the best IEP I'd ever seen—and all it had taken was the discovery of something that was right underneath our noses this entire time: Conner's voice.

Twenty-Three

L ATER THAT SAME YEAR, despite his young age, I took the same course of action with Dalton that I had with Conner. He was ten years old and I had seen him struggle with his homework and grades, but I didn't know why. It upset me that I didn't have all the answers. Were his struggles because he was missing information at school due to his combined hearing and vision loss? Did he need extra academic support, or did he have other needs that were unrelated to deafblindness? What was I missing?

The night before his IEP meeting, I lay awake, staring at a crack in the ceiling, trying to figure out how to get the IEP team to understand what was going on. Something needed to change and I had to convince them of that—but how?

Hours later, as I stood at the counter pouring my sons a cup of orange juice each, it came to me.

"Hey, Dalton," I said, putting the juice carton on the counter and turning to him.

"Yeah?" He looked up at me through his custom-made glasses. They magnified his eyes.

"How would you feel about coming to your IEP meeting with me today? You can tell your teachers how you feel at school and have a say in what they do to help."

"Okay," he chirped, fighting off prods from Hunter. They collapsed into fits of giggles as I handed them their juice cups, running over the meeting details in my mind.

In the car, I explained to Dalton that I was there to support him, but that I'd need him to be honest with his team about what was going on in the classroom and at home. I'd hoped to host the meeting at our house, so that it would be on "our turf," but that didn't work with everyone's schedules. Instead, we had to go to the district office—a gray, concrete building with heavy fire doors, and an ugly nylon carpet. I held Dalton's hand tightly as we stepped over the threshold and were greeted by a cold receptionist who pursed her glossed lips as she checked us in. We followed her directions to a stark conference room where the whole team was already seated.

My first thought was, *They've had a pre-meeting without us.* The sense of unequal power made my stomach churn. I breathed through it, for Dalton's sake.

"Hello," I said cheerfully as Dalton and I took our seats. "The reason I've called this meeting is that I've asked the IEP team for a tutor, which is something we need to discuss. I know what I'm asking for is a stretch."

"As your case manager has informed you, Dalton doesn't qualify for a tutor because he's making sufficient academic progress," the case manager stated, her tone flat.

Although I found her response unsurprising, I was hurt. Dalton's IEP team claimed to support him, but their support didn't seem to extend to advocation. It was up to me, now, I realized. Glancing at my ten-year-old son, who was still clutching my clammy palm, watching my every move. I swallowed my nausea and considered my next words carefully.

Calmly and clearly, I began by outlining my concerns for Dalton's academic and emotional welfare, explaining that actually what he needed was a teacher of the deaf and not a tutor. Knowing that the team wouldn't understand the benefits of having a teacher of the deaf on the team, I shared detailed examples and a list of the benefits.

I could tell that the case manager still wasn't convinced so I turned to Dalton, "You know how you come home every day and get frustrated with homework and end up in tears? I think the team wants to help you but needs to better understand what's going on. Do you think you could share with them what you told me?"

Dalton looks apprehensive but started in to explain how hard it was to follow the teacher in class with all the new vocabulary and larger projects.

I held my breathe as he spoke. I was so proud of Dalton. This meeting was overwhelming to me as a mom. I can't imagine how it felt to him.

When I paused for a breath, the case manager cleared her throat and addressed the team, "Thank you for being brave, Dalton, in sharing that with us." I could tell her energy shifted. She continued "I have to admit that I don't fully understand deafblindness and how to support you, but I promise you that we'll figure it out.".

What are the teams' thoughts on adding a teacher of the deaf to the team?"

The team shifted in their seats, remaining silent. I threw a pleading look in the direction of our district audiologist.

"I agree," he said, bravely. "There is research to support what she's saying."

"Thank you," Dalton said quietly. My heart swelled with pride. I could only imagine how scary it was to have a whole room of adults talking about his needs.

"I'm sorry you've been struggling," the case manager continued. "We'll make sure you get what you need."

The next day, the case manager secured approval for the district to hire an itinerant Teacher of the Deaf to work with Dalton. She called to thank me for advocating for my son's needs and for helping her better understand what she could do to help him. She also acknowledged his bravery at being there to advocate for his needs.

Now, six years after that first IEP meeting he attended, everyone is working toward the same specific goals, all of which were created with Dalton's participation.

Conner began at a college that we were thrilled he was accepted into.

Together, Todd and I drove him to campus and helped him move in. We arranged the bedding, complete with throw pillows and a soft blanket I'd bought. We hung posters on the walls, arranged Conner's books, and stocked his little refrigerator with easy snacks. We helped him find the laundry room, the bathroom, the dining hall, and all the other places he'd need to access on a daily basis. Before I knew it, we were kissing him goodbye and driving away, watching him disappear in the rearview mirror.

For a little while, things were great with Conner. He loved the independence, relishing the chance to use the skills we'd worked so hard to teach him. He was going to his classes and making headway on finding his way in the wide, wide world. But within a few weeks, he began to call home complaining of problems he was beginning to face. Although his accessible room was great in so many ways, it was set apart from the rest of the dorm rooms, which meant that he was separated from his classmates by a long hallway. He was therefore suffering socially, unable to find ways to make new friends.

Academically, Conner was coming up against teachers who preferred to take the easy route with him. At one point, he struggled to do group work in his biology lab due to a microscope that wasn't calibrated for poor eyesight. Instead of helping him troubleshoot, his teacher told him not to worry about contributing. Although the teacher thought she was helping, her solution excluded him, further isolating him from his fellow classmates when she should have contacted special services to help her make the appropriate accommodations. Magnifiers could have been ordered to help him use the tools better. A transcriber could have been employed to help him take notes from the board he was struggling to read. His group could have been placed in a quiet corner so he could hear them better. Additionally, although the campus was extremely walkable, Conner was beginning to have issues getting around.

One sunny afternoon, my phone rang after I'd just grabbed lunch on the go. When I answered, Conner was breathless on the other end of the line.

"Mom," he said, his voice strained. "I'm lost on campus. I don't know where I am."

At that moment, we both realized that something had to change. Conner had learned the necessary skills but had rarely used the white cane. Still, it was becoming apparent that it was something he *needed*. After starting to use a cane, he was soon navigating campus better, but it broke my heart to see him using a tool he'd avoided his whole life. Nothing prepares you for seeing your child use a white cane for the first time. The faces of the people around us contorted with a combination of pity and *Are you faking it? Because it sure seems like you can see something...*

Before long, due to the persistent issues with the school, Conner's grades dropped from his usual A's and B's to C's and D's. Conner had become so used to switching schools thanks to a lifetime of upheaval that he was excited to explore new schooling options. Through discussions with some fellow moms, I'd heard of a school in Upstate New York called The Rochester Institute of Technology. As hard as it was to imagine Conner being so far away, the school's services were known to be some of the best in the country. They even had a world-renowned school for the Deaf on campus. Conner applied and was accepted immediately, putting us on a plane to New York a few weeks later.

Once he was at Rochester, Conner thrived. Although he still didn't make any friends there, he began to find his way to a career he was passionate about. Fascinated by governments around the world, Conner began working toward a degree in political science. In his junior year, he even traveled to the school's campus in Kosovo and studied abroad for a semester. During that time, I'd wake every day and stare at the clock, wondering what Conner was doing a world away. When he called home, he seemed relieved that the independent life he'd always wanted was finally his. Even so, life is a rollercoaster, and as a family, we were still on a learning journey. There are still many bad days amongst the good days

Meanwhile, Dalton developed an interest in supporting and advocating for others with Usher syndrome, attending conferences, sharing his story, and raising awareness. He is in high school, looking at colleges, and wants to be a mental health counselor who specializes in helping individuals and families deal with disability.

I was so proud of both of my boys for the obstacles they overcame and all the ones they continued to tackle. While we all had to learn about Usher syndrome and how to accommodate it on our own, now, others were learning from our journey and continuing our search for solutions to daily challenges.

There were still a lot of changes to be made to make the world a more welcoming place for people with Usher syndrome, but spreading awareness was a start—and I couldn't have been prouder that my boys were leading the charge by example.

As I watched my boys grow—not just taller, but wiser—I began to see something I hadn't expected. They weren't just surviving; they were becoming. They were advocating for themselves, speaking up about what they needed, and showing the world that being deafblind didn't define their limits. In their courage, I saw the threads of every late-night worry, every meeting, every tear, and every tiny moment of joy that had carried us to this place. And as I looked at them, I realized: this wasn't just their story anymore. It was mine, too. Not the version shaped by fear or exhaustion, but the version rebuilt with presence, clarity, and grace. The hardest chapters didn't break us—they built us.

Twenty-Four

I T'S A YEAR LATER. I'm writing this from a quiet corner in Washington, D.C.—in between meetings with lawmakers, in between moments where my son and I are telling our story yet again, hoping someone truly listens this time.

It's surreal in some ways. To be here, not just as an advocate, but as a mom who's lived the hardest parts of this system. As someone who once sat on the bathroom floor, heartbroken and exhausted, wondering how I'd ever find the strength to keep going. And yet, I did. And so did my sons.

Now, they speak for themselves. They sit in the same rooms I once entered alone, using their voices to educate, to connect, to pave the way for others. Watching them—especially Dalton—share their truth with such quiet power, I feel it in my bones: it was all worth it.

Every sleepless night. Every IEP battle. Every heartbreak. Every time I stood up when I didn't think I could.

Grief hasn't left me. It still sits beside me. It flares when I see my child stumble in a hallway not built for him. When I realize, once again, how much of the world remains inaccessible. But now, right next to that grief, lives something else: purpose. Pride. Peace.

Becoming Through the Both-And

There's no neat resolution here. I didn't "get through it" and find joy waiting at the other end. What happened instead is more honest, more human: I learned to carry them both.

The ache and the awe. The sorrow and the celebration. The exhaustion and the purpose.

I became the kind of woman I used to long to be—strong in my truth, soft in my grief, grounded in my knowing. Not because I erased the hard parts, but because I brought them with me and kept going anyway.

For the Ones Who Come After

As I walk these marble halls with my son, as we speak to people who shape the systems we've spent our lives trying to navigate, I think about all the families who haven't been heard yet. The ones still waiting for someone to believe them. The ones doing everything they can just to keep their heads above water.

We speak for them. We show up for them. Because someone has to open the door wider.

And I know now: the story we've lived—imperfect, painful, resilient—is the very thing that might make it easier for someone else. That's how change happens. Slowly. Quietly. Through lived experience turned into courage.

If You're Still in It

If you're reading this and feeling that familiar ache, or the weight of not being seen—just know this: there is nothing wrong with how you're carrying your experience.

You don't need to be ready to speak about it. You don't need to feel strong every day. You don't owe anyone a version of this that makes it easier to understand.

But maybe, with time, you'll start to notice the quiet ways you've grown. The way your perspective shifts. The way you soften in places you once felt sharp. The way you've kept going, even when you weren't sure how.

That's where I am now. I still carry everything I've been through. But I also carry clarity. Connection. And the quiet confidence that my life—and my children's lives—are helping to shape something better.

And this—this chapter—is what lets me close this part of the story with a steadier heart, and a wide open hope for what comes next.

Conclusion

There were days I didn't think I'd make it. Days I cried on the bathroom floor, clutching a baby monitor in one hand and an insurance denial letter in the other. Days I smiled at school pickup while feeling like I was quietly breaking apart inside. If you've lived that dual reality—of appearing strong while feeling hollow—you'll understand what I mean when I say: this journey demanded more than I knew I had. But it also gave me more than I ever imagined was possible.

In these pages, I've told the truth of how I learned to mother in the face of uncertainty. How I became an advocate without asking to be one. How I let grief walk beside me—not to defeat me, but to remind me of what mattered most. And ultimately, how I returned to myself after years of setting my own needs aside.

The key themes of this book still hold true: the sacredness of parent intuition, the power of storytelling, the exhaustion of navigating systems that weren't built for our children, the loneliness of being "the only one," and the strength that comes from community, even when it's built one small connection at a time.

But now, I also carry new themes. Themes of reimagining. Of allowing softness after years of holding everything together. Of remembering that joy is not a betrayal of pain, but a companion to it. Of becoming whole—not because the hard parts disappeared, but because I learned how to hold them with love.

My name has changed since I first wrote this book, and so has my life. I am now Lanya Lynn Elsa. Choosing that name wasn't about forgetting who I was, but about honoring who I have become. It is a name that holds both my past and my future. It is the name I wore when I stood beside my wife, Bergen, and promised to keep choosing love and truth, over and over again.

I never imagined I'd be writing a second chapter of my life that included finding the love of my life, leaving behind what no longer served me, and stepping fully into who I am—not just as a mother, but as a soul. But here I am. And I've never felt more clear, more alive, or more at peace.

If you are reading this and wondering whether it's too late to rewrite your story—it's not.

If you are tired, afraid, or just trying to survive—please know that you are not alone.

And if you are craving a life that holds more joy, more meaning, and more truth—I hope this book reminds you that you are worthy of all of it.

This story will always be about my children, because they are my heart. But now I know that telling the truth of my own journey is also part of how I mother them. I am not just showing them how to survive hard things. I am showing them how to live with joy, to speak up with courage, and to love with their whole hearts.

To every parent, every advocate, every human becoming: you don't have to have it all figured out. You just have to keep showing up—with softness, with strength, and with a willingness to be seen.

Thank you for witnessing my story.

I'm not done writing it yet.

A new book is coming in Fall 2025—a continuation of this journey, as I reimagine the second half of my life and choose joy, love, and truth again and again.

And after that, a third book—focused entirely on parent advocacy, on how lived experience can transform systems, and on how our stories are the blueprint for change.

May you leave these pages with more light than you came with.

And may you keep choosing yourself, even when it's hard.

Acknowledgments

To Conner—thank you for making me a mom. From the very beginning, you've taught me what it means to show up with love, to be brave even when things are hard, and to keep going. You've helped me grow in ways I never expected, and I'm so proud of who you are and who you're becoming. I love you!

Dalton—you have such a big heart. You notice things most people miss, and you care deeply about others. Your sense of humor, your hugs, your questions, and your quiet strength have brought so much joy to our family. I love how you see the world and how you help me see it differently too. I love you!

Cole and Hunter—thank you for being the best brothers Conner and Dalton could ask for. You've helped in more ways than you probably realize—by jumping in, by showing up, and by just being yourselves. Your support has meant the world to both dad and me. We couldn't have done it without you, and I hope you know how much I see and appreciate everything you've brought to our family. I love you both so much!

Todd, thank you for walking beside me through so much of this journey. Our time together shaped so much of this story, and I'm grateful for the family we built and the strength we found, even in the hardest moments. While the shape of our relationship has changed, the impact of what we created together will always remain.

To all our friends and family who have lent a listening ear and a helping hand, your love and support have meant the world to us.

Companion Guide

Companion Guide Highlights

This guide is a space to pause, reflect, and begin (or continue) your own healing journey. Use these prompts in a journal, a discussion group, or simply as quiet points of reflection.

General Reflection Prompts (for any Chapter)

- What part of this chapter made you feel most seen?

- What memory or emotion surfaced as you read?

- What support do you wish you'd had at that time in your life?

- How has your story shaped your identity and strength?

Sample Chapter Prompts

Chapter 1: The Unexpected Beginning– When was the last time you were underestimated?– How did the reality of parenting differ from your expectations?

Chapter 5: Medical Realities– What do you wish doctors and nurses better understood?– Why do we feel the need to hide the hard parts?

Chapter 13: The "Us" and "Them" Divide– When did you first realize you felt different from others?– How has that sense of difference impacted your relationships?

Chapter 22: Finding Your Voice– How have you advocated for yourself or someone you love?– What helped you feel empowered to speak up?

Want the full version?

Download the full printable guide—including all chapter-by-chapter questions and journaling space—at:

Or scan the QR code below.

About the Author

Lanya Lynn Elsa, PhD (formerly Lanya McKittrick), is a writer, special education researcher, and mother of four—including two sons who are deafblind due to Usher syndrome. Her journey into advocacy began with her first son's diagnosis, pulling her into a world of IEP meetings, medical decisions, and invisible grief.

Over time, she discovered the power of storytelling—not just to raise awareness, but to heal, connect, and drive change. With a doctorate in Special Education, Lanya combines her lived experience with research to help families feel seen and systems become more compassionate.

She is actively involved in the deafblind community in many ways and is passionate about creating space for family voices in the conversations that shape policy and practice. Through her writing, speaking, and consulting, she helps others find strength in their stories and hope in the journey. Learn more at www.lanyaelsa.com